AN AGE OF EMPIRES
1200-1750

STUDENT STUDY GUIDE

Oxford University Press, Inc., publishes works that
further Oxford University's objective of excellence
in research, scholarship, and education.

Oxford   New York
Auckland   Cape Town   Dar es Salaam   Hong Kong   Karachi
Kuala Lumpur   Madrid   Melbourne   Mexico City   Nairobi
New Delhi   Shanghai   Taipei   Toronto

With offices in
Argentina   Austria   Brazil   Chile   Czech Republic   France   Greece
Guatemala   Hungary   Italy   Japan   Poland   Portugal   Singapore
South Korea   Switzerland   Thailand   Turkey   Ukraine   Vietnam

Copyright © 2005 by Oxford University Press, Inc.

Published by Oxford University Press, Inc.
198 Madison Avenue, New York, NY 10016
www.oup.com

Oxford is a registered trademark of Oxford University Press

All rights reserved. No part of this publication may be reproduced,
stored in a retrieval system, or transmitted in any form or by any means,
electronic, mechanical, photocopying, recording, or otherwise,
without the prior permission of Oxford University Press.

ISBN-13: 978-0-19-522341-5

Editor and Project Director: Jacqueline A. Ball
Education Consultant: Diane L. Brooks, Ed.D
Design: designlabnyc

Casper Grathwohl, Publisher

Dear Parents, Guardians, and Students:

This study guide has been created to increase student enjoyment and understanding of *An Age of Empires, 1200–1750*. It has been developed to help students access the text. As they do so, they can learn history and the social sciences and improve reading, language arts, and study skills.

The study guide offers a wide variety of interactive exercises to support every chapter. Parents or other family members can participate in activities labeled "With a Parent or Partner." Adults can help in other ways, too. One important way is to encourage students to create and use a history journal as they work through the exercises in the guide. The journal can simply be an off-the-shelf notebook or three-ring binder used only for this purpose. Some students might like to customize their journals with markers, colored paper, drawings, or computer graphics. No matter what it looks like, a journal is a student's very own place to organize thoughts, practice writing, and make notes on important information. It will serve as a personal report of ongoing progress that your child's teacher can evaluate regularly. When completed, it will be a source of satisfaction and accomplishment for your child.

Sincerely,

Casper Grathwohl
Publisher

This book belongs to:

_____

CONTENTS

How to Use the Student Study Guides to *The Medieval & Early Modern World*   6

Graphic Organizers   8

Reports and Special Projects   10

Chapter 1   11
Golden Khan, Golden Reins, Golden Horde: The Mongols Ride Out
In the early 13th century, the Mongol clans of Central Asia united with Genghis Khan as their leader. He led the Mongols in creating an empire that stretched from Korea to central Europe and was the largest land empire in history.

Chapter 2   15
Who's Next? The Mongols Reach Their Limit
The Mongols enlarged their empire with conquests in Asia and central Europe. They were often brutal, but the Mongols treated submissive enemies fairly well. By the middle of the 13th century, the Mongol grasp on Asia began to loosen, and in 1368, Ming forces in China overthrew the Mongols' Yuan Dynasty.

Chapter 3   19
Twice as Powerful: Poland and Lithuania Unite
In spite of their differences, Poland and Lithuania began to unite during the 14th century and became Europe's largest empire. The Renaissance supported thinkers such as Copernicus, who changed people's perception of the universe. Many factors caused the Polish and Lithuanian Commonwealth to decline in power by the 18th century.

Chapter 4   23
Troubled Times, Troubled Tsars: The Russian Empire
Russia was unified after centuries of invasions. Under the rule of tsars, it expanded into an empire. Two of the most famous tsars were Ivan the Terrible, who brutally punished his enemies, and Peter the Great, who forced Russia to modernize.

Chapter 5   27
The Real Mughals, Not the Reel Moguls: Empire in India
In the 16th and 17th centuries, a series of Mughal emperors ruled India. At its peak, the Mughal Empire encouraged trade and created beautiful art and architecture. The Mughals were Muslims, but most of them were religiously tolerant. They also granted women positions of respect.

Chapter 6   31
Triumph of the Turks: The Rise of the Ottoman Empire
The sultans, or leaders of the Ottoman Turks, defeated their enemies to form the powerful Ottoman Empire. This Islamic empire lasted more than 600 years.

Chapter 7   35
When Tents Become Towers: The Sultans Settle Down
The Ottoman Empire flourished and expanded during the reign of the sultan Suleyman, and Istanbul was established as its capital city. After Suleyman's death, ineffective rulers and other difficulties began to weaken the empire.

Chapter 8 39
Stocking the Royal Spice Cabinet: The Portuguese Empire
    Exploration and naval power were keys to the building of the Portuguese empire and control of valuable trade routes in the 1400s and 1500s. Much of what the Portuguese gained was later lost, but many changes resulted from Portugal's contact with other parts of the world, both within and outside of the empire.

Chapter 9 43
"Go Further!": Spain Expands across an Ocean
    The Catholic monarchy of Spain expanded its empire across the world and made Catholicism the dominant religion. Over time, the empire weakened because it did not develop its resources.

Chapter 10 47
The Wedding Ring Empire: Europe under the Habsburgs
    The Habsburg Empire used royal weddings to rule over parts of Central Europe for 500 years. Their devotion to Catholicism was the source of ever-deepening religious conflict.

Chapter 11 51
Teenagers Take the Throne: Manchu China
    The Manchus of northeastern China began the Qing dynasty. They tried to keep their culture intact while ruling the Chinese majority. At the height of the dynasty, the Qing rulers supported education and trade and expanded China's borders.

Library/Media Center Research Log 55

HOW TO USE THE STUDENT STUDY GUIDES TO
THE MEDIEVAL & EARLY MODERN WORLD

Each book in The Medieval & Early Modern World introduces you to compelling adventures of fascinating men and women living at an amazing time. You will meet artists and warriors, rulers and scientists, merchants, traders, and slaves. You'll experience their lives close up, through diaries, letters, poems, songs, and myths.

The events of the medieval and early modern time period changed the whole world forever. The foundations of international politics, the boundaries of countries and empires, the roots of educational and religious institutions—all were established during this rich, electrifying period. We can't fully understand our world today without understanding how it connects with these times.

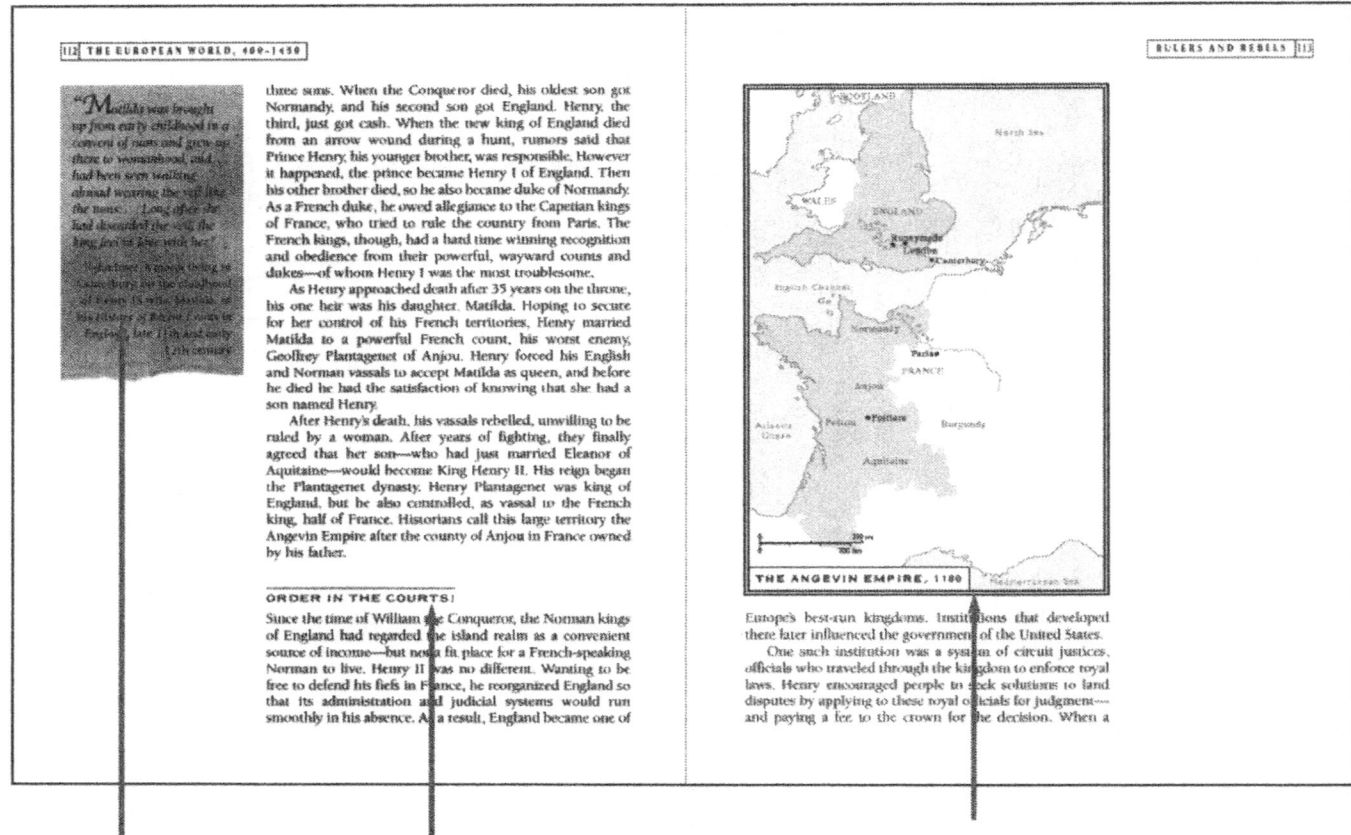

Short quotes in sidebars tell about life in the words of someone living at the time.

Subheads give clues to the content to follow.

Geography has a lot to do with history. Maps show the locations of important places and supply a geographic context for important events.

This study guide will help you as you read the books in the series. It will help you learn and enjoy history while building thinking and writing skills. And it will help you pass important tests. The sample pages below show the books' special features. But before you begin reading the book or using this guide, be sure to have a notebook or extra paper and a pen handy to make a history journal. A dictionary and thesaurus will help you too. A special tip: Before you start a new chapter, read the two-part chapter title and predict what you will learn from the chapter. Check to see if you were right at the end.

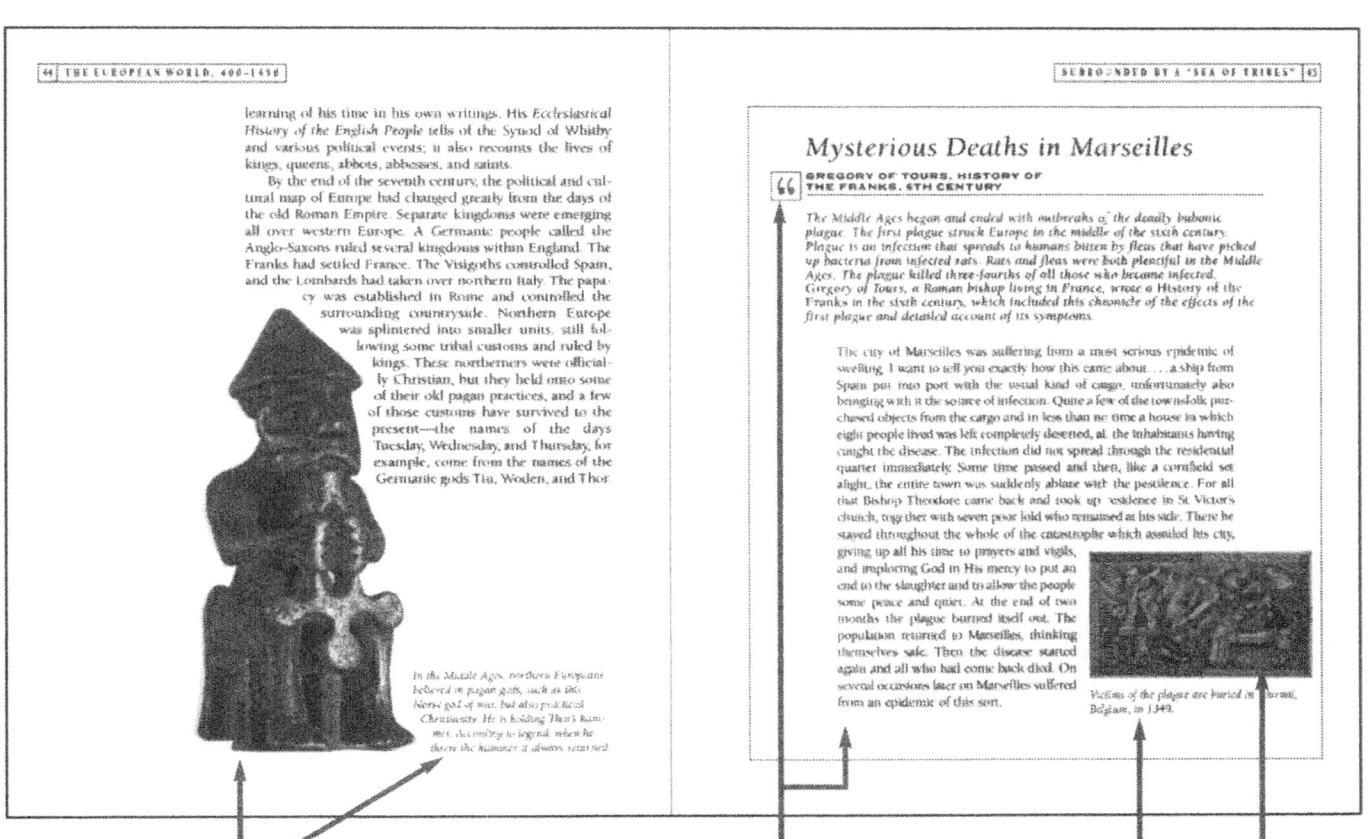

Pictures, often of artifacts, show distinctive art and design of the times. Read the captions to learn even more than is in the text.

Every chapter has a long primary source quote that takes you back in time to the scene of a significant action in a dramatic, powerful, first-person way. Look for these longer quotations marked by quotation marks followed by the source of the work.

On the next pages you will find models of graphic organizers. You will need these to do the activities for each chapter on the pages after that. Go back to the book as often as you need to.

7

GRAPHIC ORGANIZERS

As you read and study history, geography, and the social sciences, you'll start to collect a lot of information. Using a graphic organizer is one way to make information clearer and easier to understand. You can choose from different types of organizers, depending on the information.

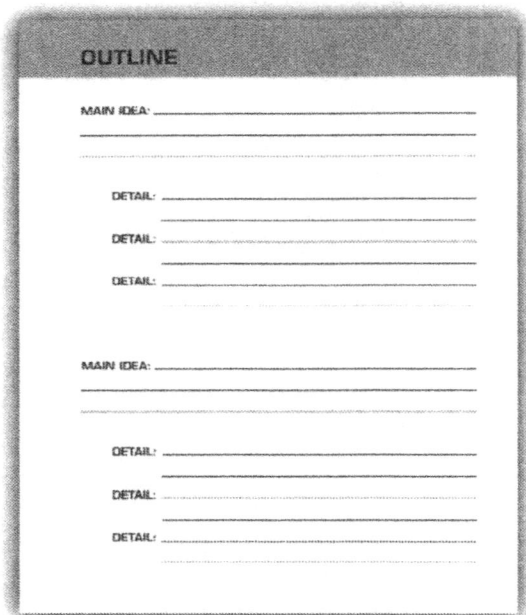

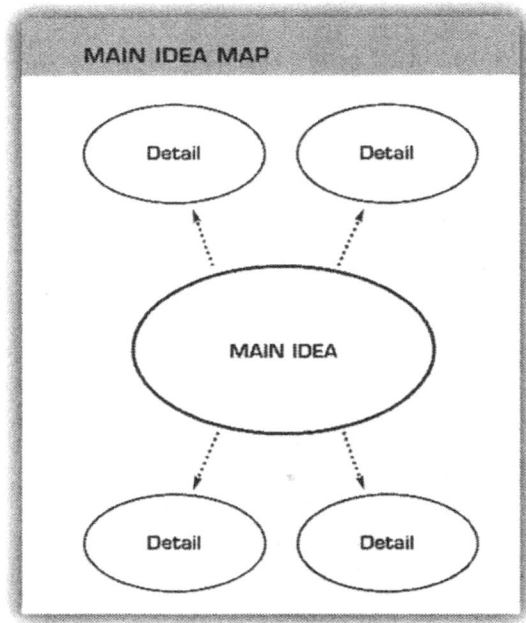

Outline
To build an outline, first identify your main idea. Write this at the top. Then, in the lines below, list the details that support the main idea. Keep adding main ideas and details as you need to.

Main Idea Map
Write down your main idea in the central circle. Write details in the connecting circles.

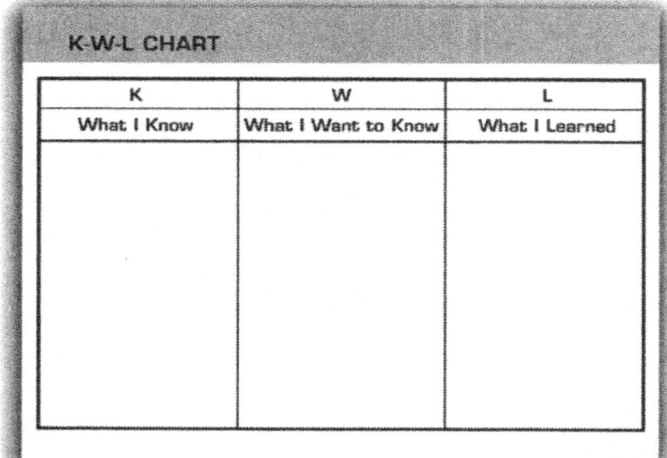

K-W-L Chart
Before you read a chapter, write down what you already know about a subject in the left column. Then write what you want to know in the center column. Then write what you learned in the last column. You can make a two-column version of this. Write what you know in the left and what you learned after reading the chapter.

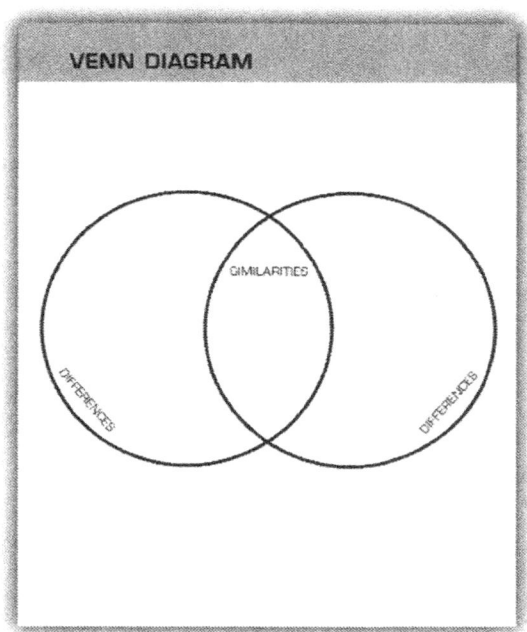

Venn Diagram
These overlapping circles show differences and similarities among topics. Each topic is shown as a circle. Any details the topics have in common go in the areas where those circles overlap. List the differences where the circles do not overlap.

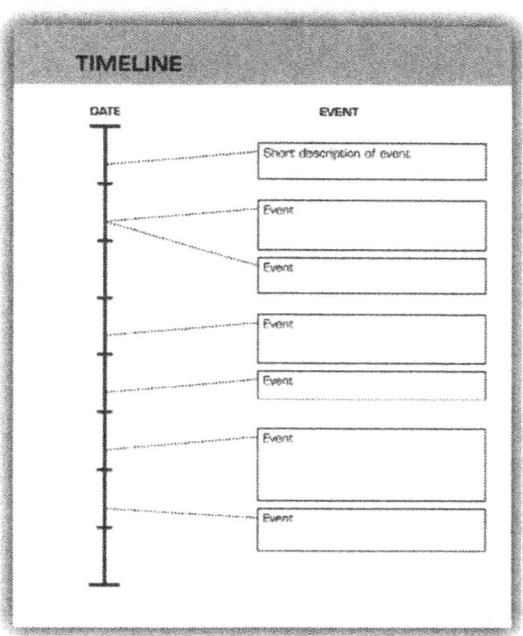

Timeline
A timeline divides a time period into equal chunks of time. Then it shows when events happened during that time. Decide how to divide up the timeline. Then write events in the boxes to the right when they happened. Connect them to the date line.

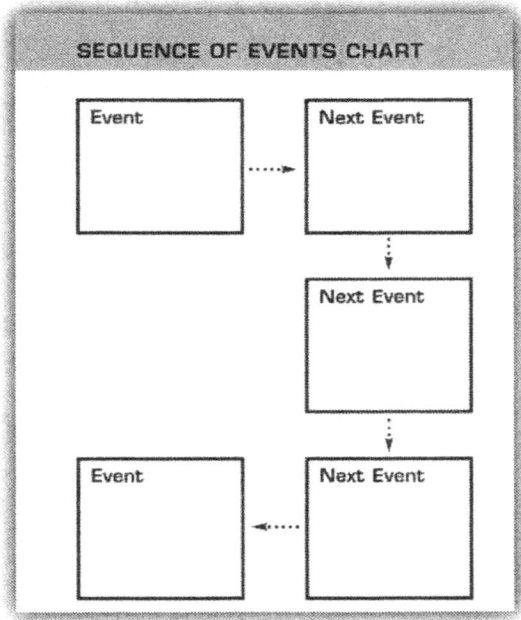

Sequence of Events Chart
Historical events bring about changes. These result in other events and changes. A sequence of events chart uses linked boxes to show how one event leads to another, and then another.

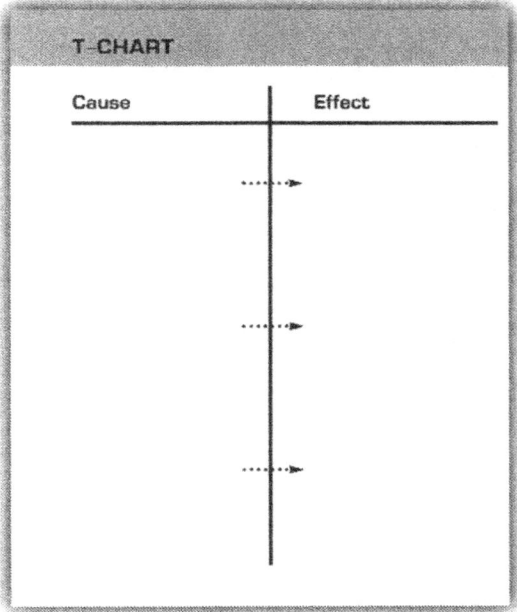

T-Chart
Use this chart to separate information into two columns. To separate causes and effects, list events, or causes, in one column. In the other column, list the change, or effect, each event brought about.

REPORTS AND SPECIAL PROJECTS

There's always more to find out about empires and early modern history. Take a look at the Further Reading section at the end of the book (pages 150–152). Here you'll find a number of books on different topics relating to this dramatic, transforming period in time. Many of them will be available in your school or local public library.

GETTING STARTED

Explore the Further Reading section for any of these reasons:
- You're curious and want to learn more about a particular topic.
- You want to do a research report on medieval history.
- You still have questions about something covered in the book.
- You need more information for a research or other classroom project.

What's the best way to find the books that will help you the most?

LOOK AT THE SUBHEADS

Most of the books in this section are organized by empire: the Manchu Empire, the Ottoman Empire, the Habsburg Empire, and so on. Within these categories, you will find biographies where you can get detailed, in-depth looks at the explorers, rulers, conquerors, and thinkers who shaped this period: Genghis Khan, Copernicus, Suleyman, Queen Isabella. You will find books that beckon you to be an explorer yourself — to be on board a ship charting new territory or be on a battlefield, witnessing a fierce fight for land and power.

LOOK AT THE BOOK TITLES

The title of a book can tell you a lot about the content inside and often give a clue about the way the content is presented. For instance, you can expect lots of pictures in *The Emperors' Album: Images of Mughal India* and *Akbar's India: Art from the Mughal City of Victory*. You can expect a focus on religion in *Peking: Temples and City Life, 1400–1900*. Wherever you see quotation marks preceding a title, you can expect primary source material. Skim the titles for help in narrowing your focus and for the treatments with the most appeal to you.

LOOK FOR GENERAL REFERENCES

This section also lists general books, which are useful starting points for further research. General Works on Empires and Early Modern History lists titles that provide a broad overview of the Age of Empires, 1200–1750. Judge by the titles which books will be the most useful to you. Other references include:
- Dictionaries
- Encyclopedias
- Atlases

OTHER RESOURCES

Information comes in all kinds of formats. Use the book to learn about primary sources. Go to the library for videos, DVDs, and audio materials. And don't forget about the Internet.

AUDIO-VISUAL MATERIALS

Your school or local library can offer documentary videos and DVDs on the Age of Empires, as well as audio materials. If you have access to a computer, explore the sites listed in the section titled Websites (page 153) for some good jumping-off points. These are organized by topic, with brief descriptions of what you'll find on the site. Many websites list additional reading, as well as other Internet links you can visit.

What you've found out about *An Age of Empires* so far is just a beginning. Learn more to be part of an ongoing adventure.

CHAPTER 1
GOLDEN KHAN, GOLDEN REINS, GOLDEN HORDE: THE MONGOLS RIDE OUT

CHAPTER SUMMARY

In the early 13th century, the Mongol clans of Central Asia united with Genghis Khan as their leader. He led the Mongols in creating an empire that stretched from Korea to central Europe and was the largest land empire in history.

ACCESS

As you read the chapter, review each main idea listed below. Add details that support the main idea on the lines provided. Chapter 1 also describes the Mongol people and their horses. You may use the outline graphic organizer on page 8 to note main ideas and details about these additional topics.

MAIN IDEA: Genghis Khan was a hard man from a hard background.

DETAIL: _____

DETAIL: _____

DETAIL: _____

MAIN IDEA: Many factors made the Mongol army effective.

DETAIL: _____

DETAIL: _____

DETAIL: _____

MAIN IDEA: An increase in trade balanced some of the destruction caused by the Mongols.

DETAIL: _____

DETAIL: _____

DETAIL: _____

CAST OF CHARACTERS

State why each character was important.

Batu (bah-TOO) _____

Genghis Khan (GENG-guhs KAHN) _____

Khubilai Khan (KOO-buh-lie KAHN) _____

WHAT HAPPENED WHEN?

In your history journal, make a timeline like the one on page 9. Fill in these dates and the events that happened on each one:

    1206   1220   1227   1279

WORD BANK

conquered   maneuvers   campaign   brutality   invincibility   coalition   ambush

Choose words from the Word Bank to complete the sentences. One word is not used at all.

1. The Mongols used some of the same _____ in hunting and in war.
2. The Mongols would set up an _____ to attack unprotected armies.
3. Women often accompanied men on a military _____.
4. The Mongols _____ some of the most literate societies of their time.
5. The Europeans united at Liegnitz, but the Mongols defeated the _____.
6. Because the Mongols kept winning battles, they gained a reputation for _____.

WORD PLAY

In a dictionary, look up the word you did not use. Write a sentence using that word.

_____
_____

CRITICAL THINKING

SEQUENCE

Sometimes writers use dates and words such as *first, before, at the beginning, then, after, once,* and *later* to indicate the order in which events occur. These words are called signal words. Circle the signal words in the sentences below. Then write the adjective that comes from the same root. Write the number of each event in the correct order in the sequence diagram to show the order in which the Mongols built their empire.

1. Then Genghis and his sons defeated the Khwarazm Empire.
2. At last, Khubilai Khan unified China.
3. The first attacks of the Mongols went east.
4. Genghis Khan's son Jochi and his grandson Batu defeated the Russians.
5. Genghis Khan gained control of the clans of Central Asia.

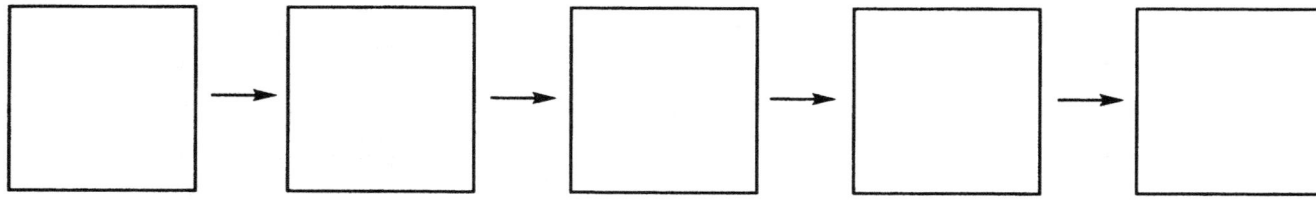

WORKING WITH PRIMARY SOURCES

Read the sidebar from Student Edition page 22, from *The History of the World Conqueror*. In it Persian historian Juvaini laments the Mongol destruction of the Iranian irrigation system.

> With one stroke a world which billowed with fertility was laid desolate, and the regions thereof became a desert, with the greater part of the living dead, and their skin and bones crumbling dust, and the mighty were humbled.

IDENTIFYING FIGURATIVE LANGUAGE AND POINT OF VIEW

Answer the following questions on the lines provided.

1. What problem did the destruction of the Iranian irrigation system cause?

2. Do you think that Juvaini viewed the Mongols as destroyers of civilizations or as protectors of flourishing trade networks? Explain.

3. *Hyperbole* is a figure of speech in which exaggeration is used for emphasis or effect. What example of hyperbole does Juvaini use?

4. Why do you think that Juvaini chose to use hyperbole?

WRITE ABOUT IT

In your history journal, write several paragraphs describing a place or event that has changed in a remarkable way. Use at least one example of hyperbole in your account.

HISTORY JOURNAL

Don't forget to share your history journal with your classmates, and ask if you can see what their journals look like. You might be surprised—and get some new ideas.

ALL OVER THE MAP

Directions

Follow the steps below to show the destruction and improvements caused by the Mongols as they built their empire.

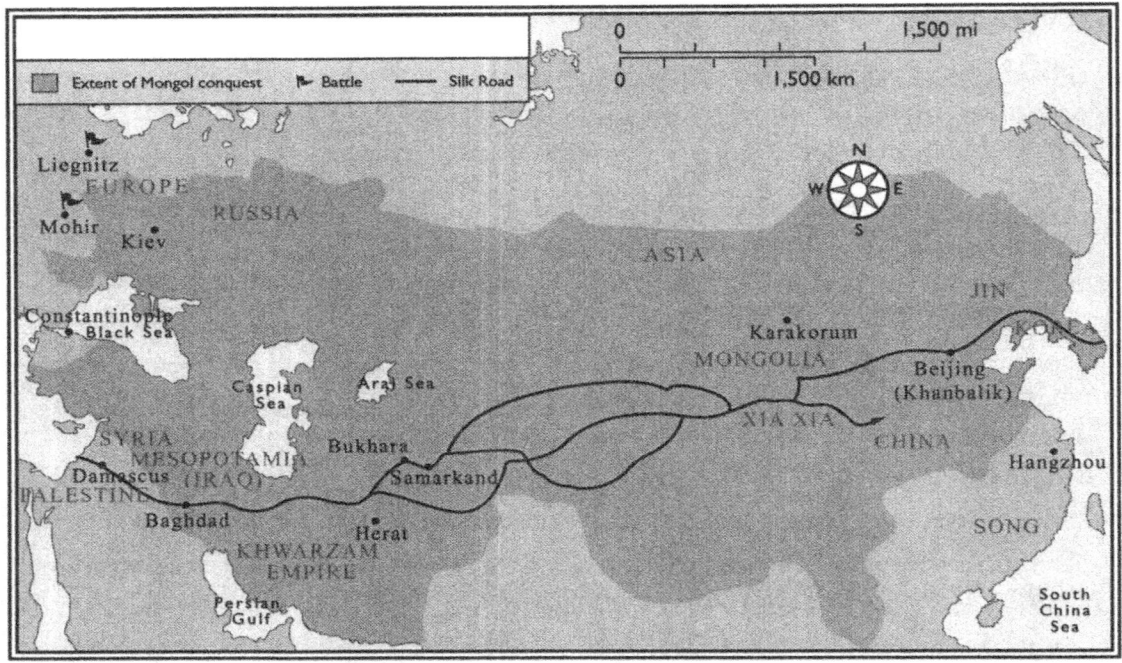

MAP LEGEND

- Scan Student Edition pages 20–24 to find information on the destruction and improvements caused by the Mongols as they built their empire.
- Make a list of the destruction and improvements caused by the Mongols. When possible, note where and when the destruction and improvements occurred.
- Make a small drawing, or icon, to represent each type of destruction and improvement. For example, you might show a stick figure of a person to represent large numbers of people killed in battle.
- Draw each icon where it belongs on the map. For example, you could add a stick figure of a person next to Kiev to show that many people were killed there in battle.
- When possible, add a date next to the icon to show when the destruction or improvement occurred.
- Make a legend for your map showing what each icon stands for.
- Give your map a title that explains what the map shows.

CHAPTER 2
WHO'S NEXT?: THE MONGOLS REACH THEIR LIMIT

CHAPTER SUMMARY
The Mongols enlarged their empire with conquests in Asia and central Europe. They were often brutal, but the Mongols treated submissive enemies fairly well. By the middle of the 13th century, the Mongol grasp on Asia began to loosen, and in 1368, Ming forces in China overthrew the Mongols' Yuan Dynasty.

ACCESS
Complete the main idea map below by adding details about Khubilai Khan's personality and accomplishments. Create a similar main idea map (page 8) to note details about Timur. Use your completed graphic organizers to help you recall how these leaders were alike and different.

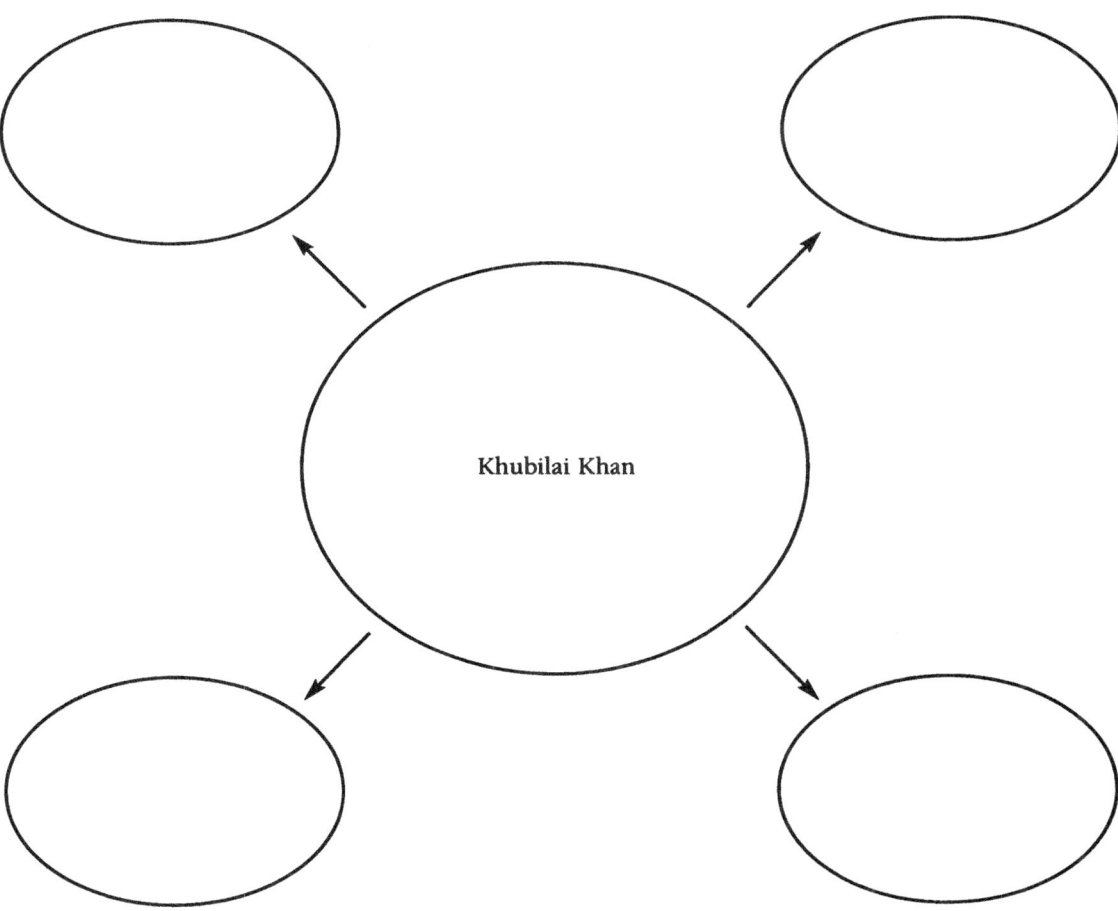

AN AGE OF EMPIRES, 1200–1750   **15**

CAST OF CHARACTERS

Write a few sentences about why each character was important.

Marco Polo _____
_____
_____

Timur (TEE-mer) _____
_____
_____

WORD BANK

refugees   nomads   administrators   allies   rivals   deception   demise   strategists

Each of the clues on the left describes people. In the space provided, write the word from the Word Bank that matches each clue. Two words are not used.

Clue	Word
These people might work in the offices of your local government.	1. _____
These people might join together to help one another in time of war.	2. _____
During a war, these people might be forced to leave their homes to find a safer place to live.	3. _____
These people often move from place to place, seeking new lands.	4. _____
These people compete against each other for a common goal, such as winning a battle.	5. _____
These people have great skill in planning how to reach a goal, such as winning a war	6. _____

WORD PLAY

Look up the two words you did not use. What is similar about them?
_____

Write a sentence that suggests the meaning of each word.
_____
_____

CHAPTER 2

CRITICAL THINKING
CAUSE AND EFFECT

As you read Chapter 2, think about how the following causes led to certain events. Fill in the chart with the correct effects.

CAUSE (A reason)	EFFECT (What happens as a result)
1. The Mongols wanted Korea's rice, soldiers, and the naval power.	
2. Huge storms destroyed two Mongol invasion fleets on their way to Japan.	
3. The Russians, Koreans, and Chinese wanted to strengthen their nations against future attacks.	
4. Ming forces gained strength in the middle of the 14th century.	

WORKING WITH PRIMARY SOURCES

Read the banner text on Student Edition page 31 and answer the questions that follow.

> It is better to be at the right place with one hundred men than to be somewhere else with ten thousand.
> —Timur the Lame, advice about moving troops, late 1390s

1. What does Timur's advice show about his skills as a strategist?

2. Describe a situation in which Timur might have given this advice about moving troops.

IN YOUR OWN WORDS

Part of the beauty of Timur's statement is that it would be difficult to disagree with his simple advice. Think about some advice that you could give about something you know well. In your history journal, write a statement of your own advice, using the style of Timur's statement:

It is better to _____ than to _____.

Explain the reasoning behind your advice in two or three paragraphs.

ALL OVER THE MAP

Directions

Follow the steps below to complete the map.

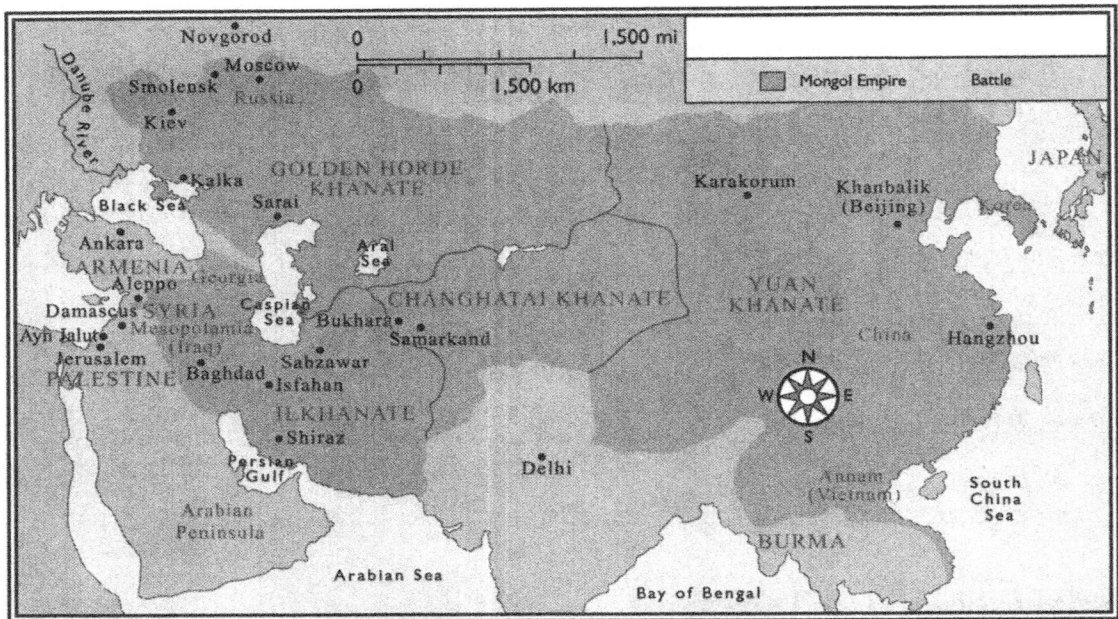

MAP LEGEND

- Use a colored pencil to shade the area of the Golden Horde controlled by Batu.
- Use a second color to shade the area of the Yuan Dynasty controlled by Khubilai Khan.
- Reread the description of Timur's conquests on Student Edition pages 34–36. Make a list of the places he controlled.
- Use a third color to shade the area around the areas controlled by Timur.
- Add the colors you used for shading to the map legend, and explain what each color represents.
- Give the map a title that explains what it shows.

CHAPTER 3
TWICE AS POWERFUL: POLAND AND LITHUANIA UNITE

CHAPTER SUMMARY
In spite of their differences, Poland and Lithuania began to unite during the 14th century and became Europe's largest empire. The Renaissance supported thinkers such as Copernicus, who changed peoples' perception of the universe. Many factors caused the Polish and Lithuanian Commonwealth to decline in power by the 18th century.

ACCESS
Chapter 3 discusses how Poland and Lithuania united and became a powerful empire. As you read the chapter, show the countries' similarities and differences by adding details to complete the Venn diagram.

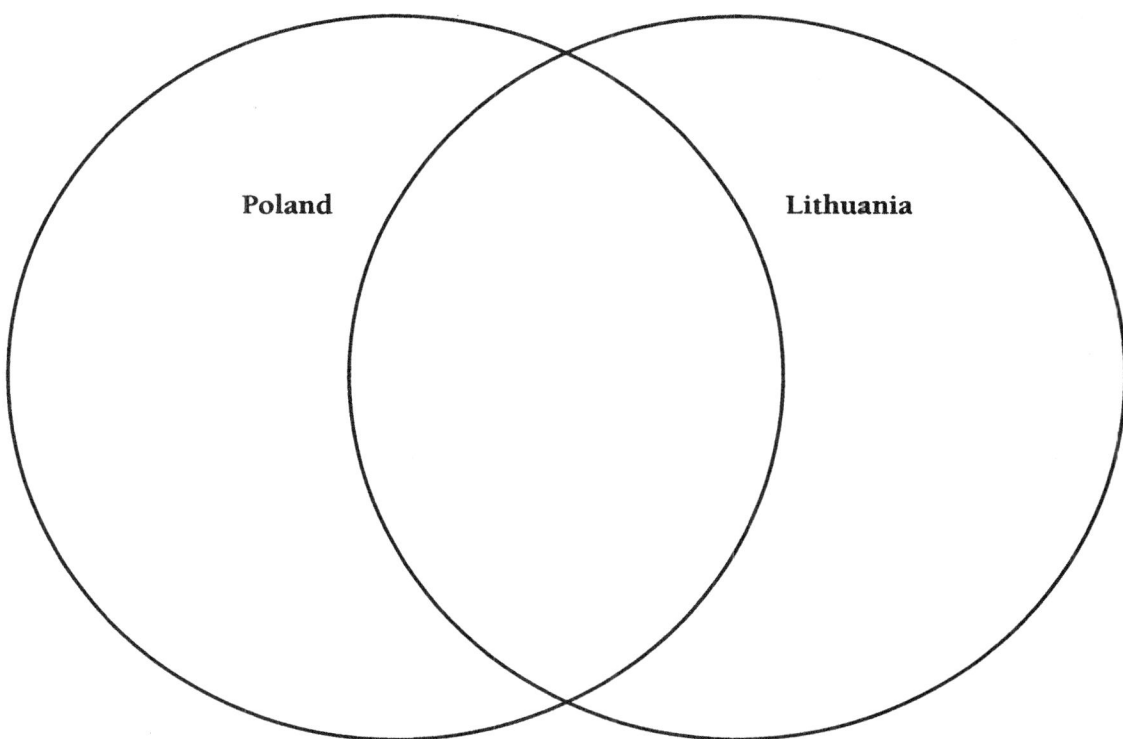

CAST OF CHARACTERS

Explain the role each character played in Polish and Lithuanian history.

Jogaila (JOH-gai-luh) _____

_____

Jadwiga (JAH-dwee-guh) _____

_____

Vytautas (vih-TAO-tuhs) _____

_____

Nicolaus Copernicus (kuh-PER-nih-khus) _____

_____

Jan Sobieski (SOH-bee-skee) _____

_____

WORD BANK

partition   controversial   pagan   modernizing   clan   heretics

Choose words or terms from the Word Bank to complete the sentences. Two words are not used at all.

1. The Lithuanian religion was seen as _____ by the Poles because it was non-Christian.
2. In 1772, the Polish and Lithuanian Commonwealth lost some of its land to more powerful countries in what became known as the First _____.
3. While magnates seized control of land in Poland, neighboring countries were growing in strength and power by _____ their militaries.
4. The *szlachta* elected leaders from within a _____ of associated individuals.

WORD PLAY

Look up the words you did not use in the dictionary. Write one sentence that includes both words.

_____

CRITICAL THINKING
MAKING GENERALIZATIONS

Generalizations are broad statements that can be supported by facts or observations. Making generalizations can help you put many related details into a statement that expresses a larger idea.

Review what you have learned about the work of Nicolaus Copernicus and complete the statements in the table below.

FACTS AND OBSERVATIONS
Copernicus determined that _____
Most people at the time believed that _____
His book was placed on a list _____.

Use the information from the table to make a generalization about the speed at which Copernicus' findings became accepted by most people.

WORKING WITH PRIMARY SOURCES

Read this poem from the sidebar on Student Edition page 41. It was written by the Polish poet Krzysztof Opalinski in the 17th century. Then answer the questions that follow.

> As I understand it, God does not punish Poland for nothing.
> But chiefly for the harsh oppression visited on the serfs.
> For God's sake, have you Poles lost your minds completely?
> Your whole welfare, your supply of food, the wealth you amass,
> All derives from your serfs. It is their hands which feed you.

1. Is the poet addressing the magnates or the farmers who work for them? How can you tell?

2. Why does the poet believe that God has chosen to punish Poland?

3. Write a sentence that summarizes what the poet is trying to say in the last two lines.

ALL OVER THE MAP

Directions

Follow the steps below to complete the map. (Be sure to refer to the book frequently in this exercise and all others).

- Review the religious beliefs held by Poland and Lithuania in the early 1300s.
- Choose a color to represent Christian beliefs, and use it to color that country's name on the map.
- Choose another color to represent pagan beliefs, and use it to color that country's name.
- Create a map legend and tell what these colors represent.
- Write *Jadwiga* and *Jogaila* next to their native country's names.
- Place an X next to the place where the Polish and Lithuanian forces defeated the Teutonic Knights on July 19, 1410. Add this symbol and what it represents to the map legend.
- Circle the name of the country and region that the Commonwealth battled in the Great Northern Wars. Add this symbol and what it represents to the map legend.
- Place an XX next to where Jan Sobieski successfully defeated the Ottomans in 1683. Add this symbol and what it represents to the map legend.
- Give your map a title that explains what it shows.

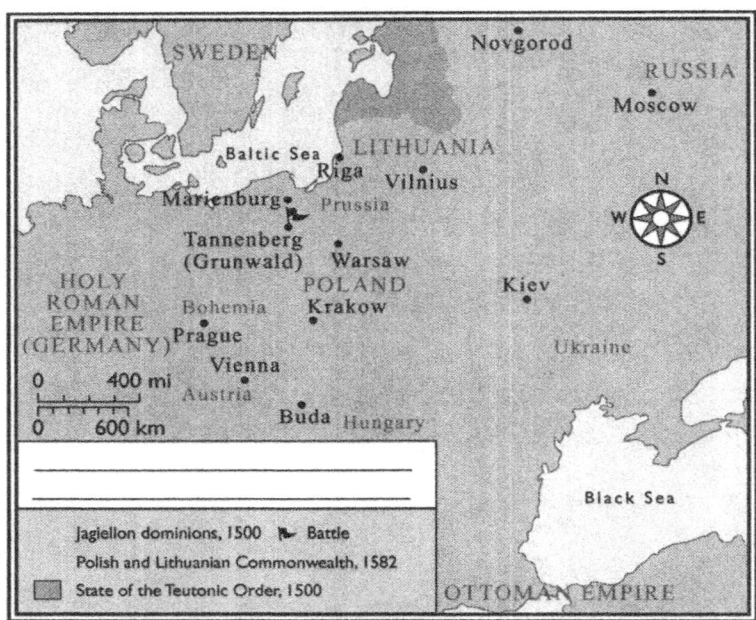

MAP LEGEND

CHAPTER 4
TROUBLED TIMES, TROUBLED TSARS: THE RUSSIAN EMPIRE

CHAPTER SUMMARY

Russia was unified after centuries of invasions. Under the rule of tsars, it expanded into an empire. Two of the most famous tsars were Ivan the Terrible, who brutally punished his enemies, and Peter the Great, who forced Russia to modernize.

ACCESS

To organize information about how the Russian Empire developed, use the cause and effect chart below. As you read each section, review the causes in the first column. Add the effect each event brought about in the second column.

CAUSE	EFFECT
1. The Russians wanted to withstand Mongol and Tartar threats.	
2. Ivan the Terrible captured the cities of Kazan and Astrakhan.	
3. Ivan began to see enemies everywhere.	
4. Alexis wanted to modernize the army.	
5. The Old Believers fought against the tsars' modernization efforts.	
6. The reforming tsars wanted to form a stronger central government.	
7. Peter the Great observed how western women were treated.	
8. Peter the Great wanted to improve education for men.	
9. Peter the Great wanted a western city on the Balkan Sea.	

CAST OF CHARACTERS

In your history journal, write a sentence describing one significant action taken by each Russian ruler below.

Ivan the Terrible   Alexis   Sophia   Peter the Great

WORD BANK

steppe   tsar   boyars   *oprichniki*   *strelsty*   *terem*

Choose words from the Word Bank to complete the sentences. One word is not used at all.

1. Upper-class women were expected to live in the _____.

2. The Russian _____ had absolute power.

3. The _____ rebelled against the changes in the military.

4. The _____ chose Mikhail Romanov to rule Russia after Ivan the Terrible's death.

5. Ivan the Terrible used the _____ to punish his enemies.

WORD PLAY

Look up the word that you did not use in the dictionary. Write a sentence that describes what it is like and where it can be found in Russia.

_____

WITH A PARENT OR PARTNER

The word *tsar*, or *czar*, comes from the name of the Roman leader Julius Caesar. Go to a website such as www.askoxford.com/worldofwords/wordfrom/bell/ to find out about the people whose names were turned into these words: *Fahrenheit, sandwich, diesel engine, saxophone,* and *chauvinism*. Talk about what you learn with a parent or a partner. List some things you could name after yourself in your history journal.

CRITICAL THINKING
MAKE GENERALIZATIONS

A generalization is a statement that shows how a group of facts are related. They sometimes include such terms as *most, many, some,* or *usually*.

FACTS	GENERALIZATION
Ivan the Terrible killed his son. Peter the Great killed his son. Both rulers tortured and killed their enemies. Both rulers had absolute power.	Some rulers with absolute power have no safeguards against being cruel.

1. Is the generalization above valid? Explain your answer.

   _____

   _____

2. State two or three facts about Russia's struggles to become Westernized.

   _____

   _____

3. What generalization can you make about Russia's struggles to become Westernized?

   _____

   _____

WORKING WITH PRIMARY SOURCES

Read the quotation from Ivan the Terrible's will, written in 1572. It appears on Student Edition page 52.

> My body grows weak, my soul is sick.... All have returned me evil for good, hatred for love.

IDENTIFYING POINT OF VIEW

Remember that after Ivan IV's wife died, he assumed that he had enemies everywhere, and he brutally punished them. He also caused the death of his son, and, indirectly, his daughter-in-law and unborn grandchild.

1. How does Ivan the Terrible feel about his life?

   _____
   _____
   _____

2. What experiences in his life might have led him to write this statement?

   _____
   _____
   _____

3. Ivan's wife died by chance, under mysterious circumstances. How did this event shape Russian history?

   _____
   _____
   _____

4. Does what you learn about Ivan the Terrible from this quotation alter your view of him? Explain.

   _____
   _____
   _____

WRITE ABOUT IT

Ivan is known to history as "the Terrible," and Peter is known as "the Great." Make a two-column chart listing actions of each man that supports each nickname. Then, is there one adjective that sums you up? You may want to check a thesaurus to help you explore the possibilities. In your history journal explain your choice, and give reasons why it would be an appropriate title. Write a short autobiographical sketch titled with your name and your adjective, explaining why it fits.

ALL OVER THE MAP

Directions:

Follow the directions below to compare historical maps.

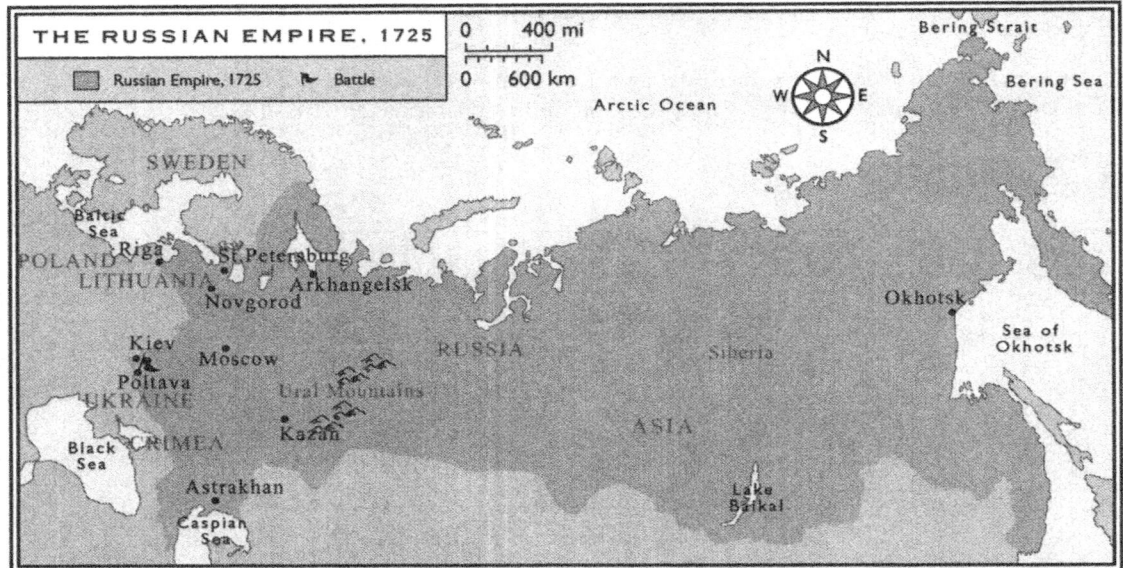

- Compare the map of The Russian Empire, 1725 with another historical map in *An Age of Empires*. Choose a map that is from the same general time period.
- On the lines below, write five questions that compare the two maps. Base the questions on the information shown here and on that map.
- When writing your questions, you might
    * compare the size of the territories.
    * compare the location and types of physical features in the empires.
    * compare the locations of major cities.
- Write the answers to your questions on a separate sheet of paper.
- Exchange your questions with a partner to answer. Then check to see if your partner answered your questions correctly.

1. _____
2. _____
3. _____
4. _____
5. _____

CHAPTER 5: THE REAL MUGHALS, NOT THE REEL MOGULS: EMPIRE IN INDIA

CHAPTER SUMMARY

In the 16th and 17th centuries, a series of Mughal emperors ruled India. At its peak, the Mughal Empire encouraged trade and created beautiful art and architecture. The Mughals were Muslims, but most of them were religiously tolerant. They also granted women positions of respect.

ACCESS

Chapter 5 describes three major Mughal emperors: Babur, Akbar, and Aurangzeb. As you read the chapter, review the main idea about each emperor shown below. Add details that support the main idea on the lines provided. Use your history journal if you need more room.

MAIN IDEA: Babur, the founder of the Mughal Empire, was a determined warrior and a great leader.

DETAIL: _____

DETAIL: _____

DETAIL: _____

MAIN IDEA: Akbar, the grandson of Babur, was the most gifted of all the Mughal emperors.

DETAIL: _____

DETAIL: _____

DETAIL: _____

MAIN IDEA: Aurangzeb, the grandson of Akbar, had a sour disposition and was intolerant of non-Muslim religions.

DETAIL: _____

DETAIL: _____

DETAIL: _____

CAST OF CHARACTERS

Write a few sentences about why each character was important. Use your history journal if you need more room.

Akbar (AHK-bahr) _____

Aurangzeb (oh-rahng-ZEHB) _____

Babur ("The Tiger") (BAH-ber) _____

WORD BANK

pomp   tyrant   rebellions   sultanate   artillery   sovereigns   diplomacy

Choose words from the Word Bank to complete the sentences. One word is not used.

1. The emperor was a _____ who few people dared to question.

2. Queens, kings, emperors, and sultans might also be called _____.

3. Enemy _____ included guns and cannons.

4. The ceremony was full of _____ with displays of gold and jewels.

5. The emperor decided to use _____ to reach an agreement with the neighboring country.

6. _____ are one way to overthrow an unjust ruler.

WORD PLAY

Write a sentence using the word that you did not use.

_____

CRITICAL THINKING

CAUSE AND EFFECT

The reason that something happens is called a *cause*. The thing that happens is called the *effect*. Fill in the chart with the correct causes and effects.

CAUSE	EFFECT
1. Akbar was a Muslim, but he wanted to promote religious tolerance.	THEREFORE, he _____.
2. BECAUSE _____,	Akbar needed someone to read to him books from his huge library.
3. BECAUSE Shah Jahan so loved his wife and mourned her death,	he wanted to honor her by _____.
4. Shah Jahan supported a son who didn't succeed in becoming the next emperor.	THEREFORE, _____.
5. Aurangzeb lacked the religious tolerance of his grandfather, Akbar.	AS A RESULT, he _____.
6. BECAUSE _____,	the Mughals can be credited with leaving behind lasting achievements.
7. BECAUSE Mughal women were generally better educated than their brothers and husbands,	they often _____.
8. The Mughals failed to use their wealth to advance their country's technology or educational facilities.	AS A RESULT, _____.

WORKING WITH PRIMARY SOURCES

Read the following quotations from Akbar. They appear in wide banners on Student Edition pages 67 and 68. Check a dictionary to help you understand any unfamiliar words. Then answer the questions that follow with complete sentences.

> We associate at convenient seasons with learned men of all religions and thus derive profit from their exquisite discourses and exalted aspirations.
>
> A monarch should be ever intent on conquest, otherwise his enemies rise in arms against him. The army should be exercised in warfare, lest from want of training they become self-indulgent.

IDENTIFYING POINT OF VIEW

1. What value does Akbar see in meeting with a variety of learned men?

2. For what reasons does Akbar think he needs continue to conquer other nations?

3. How do the quotations show different aspects of Akbar's personality?

4. How do the quotations show similar aspects of Akbar's personality?

WRITE ABOUT IT

Do you think Akbar's quotation about the need for continual conquest is right? Was conquering other nations the only way he could maintain his power and keep his army ready to defend the empire? In your history journal, write a paragraph on the lines below to share and explain your answers.

GROUP TOGETHER

Wouldn't it be interesting to know what other students think about Ancient Egyptian religious beliefs? Get a few friends together and ask your teacher to help you organize a discussion group at school. Have one person take notes and another person present the group's ideas to the class.

AN AGE OF EMPIRES, 1200–1750

ALL OVER THE MAP

Directions

Follow the steps below to complete the map.

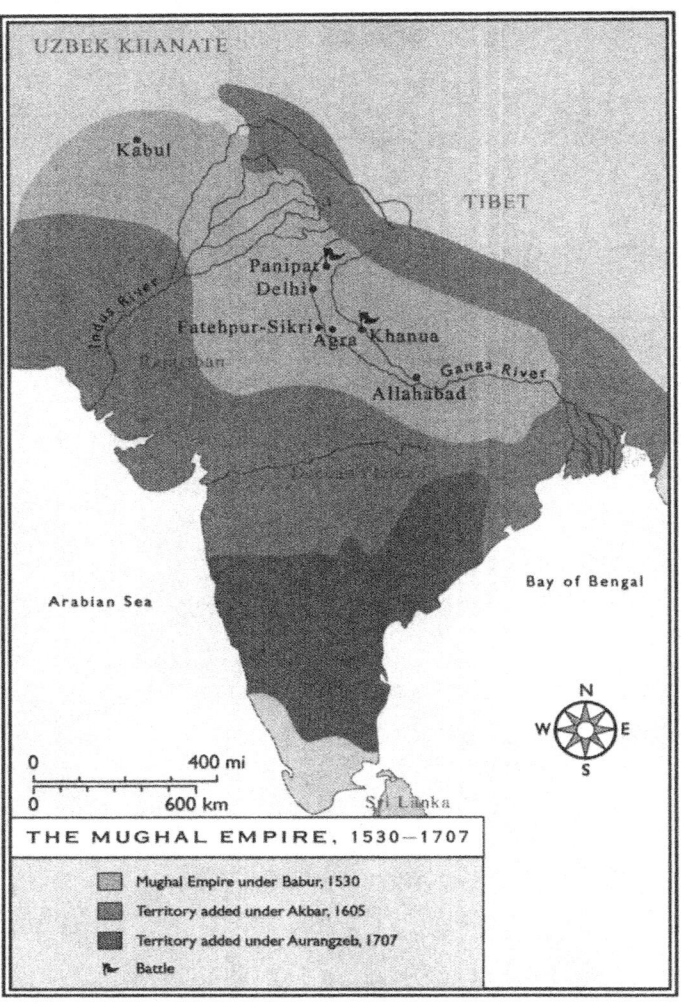

- Scan Chapter 5, and do any additional research needed to find the locations of the following Mughal buildings:
    * The Red Fort
    * the Jami Mosque
    * the Taj Mahal
- Create an icon, or small drawing, to represent each building.
- Add your icon to the map to show the location of each building.
- Add your icons to the map legend, along with an explanation of what they represent.

Describe the route you would follow to visit the three buildings.

_____
_____
_____
_____

CHAPTER 6: TRIUMPH OF THE TURKS: THE RISE OF THE OTTOMAN EMPIRE

CHAPTER SUMMARY

The sultans, or leaders of the Ottoman Turks, defeated their enemies to form the powerful Ottoman Empire. This Islamic empire lasted more than 600 years.

ACCESS

Chapter 6 describes the rule of important sultans and explains different aspects of Ottoman society. As you read the chapter, review the main ideas in the outline below. Add details that support the main idea on the lines provided.

MAIN IDEA: The Ottoman Empire was full of contradictions.

DETAIL: _____

DETAIL: _____

DETAIL: _____

MAIN IDEA: The Ottoman Turks ruled by the sword.

DETAIL: _____

DETAIL: _____

DETAIL: _____

MAIN IDEA: The Ottoman Turks sacked Constantinople.

DETAIL: _____

DETAIL: _____

DETAIL: _____

CAST OF CHARACTERS

1. Describe each person and tell why he received his nickname. Use complete sentences.

    Beyazit (bay-AH-zeet), "the Thunderbolt" _____

    _____

    Mehmet II (meh-MEHT), "the Conqueror" _____

    _____

2. Write about Timur's conflict with Beyazit.

    _____

    _____

WORD BANK

sultan   harem   Valide Sultan   *devsirme*   Ulema   *dhimmis*

Choose words from the Word Bank to complete the sentences. One word is not used at all.

1. The Ottomans called the Jews and Christians _____.

2. The Turks took Christian children as slaves in a gathering called the _____.

3. A woman who was the _____ often had much power.

4. Muslim women lived in a part of the house called the _____.

5. The _____ could officially remind the Ottoman rulers of their duties.

WORD PLAY

Look up the word that you did not use in the dictionary. Compare and contrast a person in this position with a United States president. Use complete sentences.

_____

_____

_____

_____

WITH A PARENT OR PARTNER

The vocabulary words *sultan* and *harem* are part of the English language, but they are borrowed from Arabic words. With a parent or a partner, look up the origins (etymologies) of these other words that come from Arabic and make up riddles about them: *alcove, algebra, amber, cipher, garbage,* and *mattress.* Example: You throw me away, every day, but I'm always back tomorrow (*garbage*). Use your riddles to test classmates' understanding of the words.

CRITICAL THINKING

MAKING COMPARISONS AND CONTRASTS

To make a comparison, look for how two things are alike. To show contrast, look for how two things are different. In your history journal, write a paragraph in which you contrast the Byzantine and Ottoman rule of Constantinople. Be sure to use signal words (such as *instead, but, on the other hand, unlike*) to help highlight the contrasts you describe.

WHAT HAPPENED WHEN?

For each of the following dates, identify an event that occurred or describe the period of time and write it below. Then use the Timeline graphic organizer (page 9) to create a timeline that shows how the dates are related to one another.

1387 _____

1396 _____

1402 _____

1453 _____

1566–1666 _____

WORKING WITH PRIMARY SOURCES

IDENTIFYING POINT OF VIEW

The Habsburg family ruled the Austrian Empire from 1282 to 1918. The height of the empire lasted from the end of the 1400s through the reign of Charles V, who died in 1558. During this time the Habsburg rulers struggled to protect their lands in central Europe against the Ottoman Turks.

Read the following quotation from Student Edition page 78. It is a quotation from the Habsburg Ambassador Ghiselin de Busbecq during the 16th century.

> The Turkish armies are like powerful rivers swelled by rain which cause infinite destruction when they find ways of undermining the dikes which hold them back and rush into the breach.

1. To what does the ambassador compare the Turkish armies?

   _____

   _____

2. What word signals the comparison?

   _____

   _____

3. Why do you think the ambassador felt threatened by the Ottoman Turks?

   _____

   _____

4. Does this quotation express an opinion or a fact? How can you tell?

   _____

   _____

5. How could you verify the power of the Turkish army?

   _____

   _____

6. What information might have changed the ambassador's view of the Turks?

   _____

   _____

WRITE ABOUT IT

In your history journal, write a simile about the Ottoman Empire or the Turkish army. Share it with a partner and explain why you made that particular comparison.

ALL OVER THE MAP

Directions

Follow the steps below to complete the map. Then answer the question that follows.

- Scan the chapter to find information on the key battles shown on the map here.
- Make a list of the dates and the outcomes.
- Make a small icon for each winner. For example, you can use a different-colored letter or crown corresponding to the winning sultans.
- Draw each icon on the map, with the dates.
- Make a legend for your map showing what each icon stands for.

Use your map to draw conclusions about the expansion of the empire, based on the dates and battle outcomes. Explain what the map shows about the Ottoman Empire.

_____

_____

_____

_____

_____

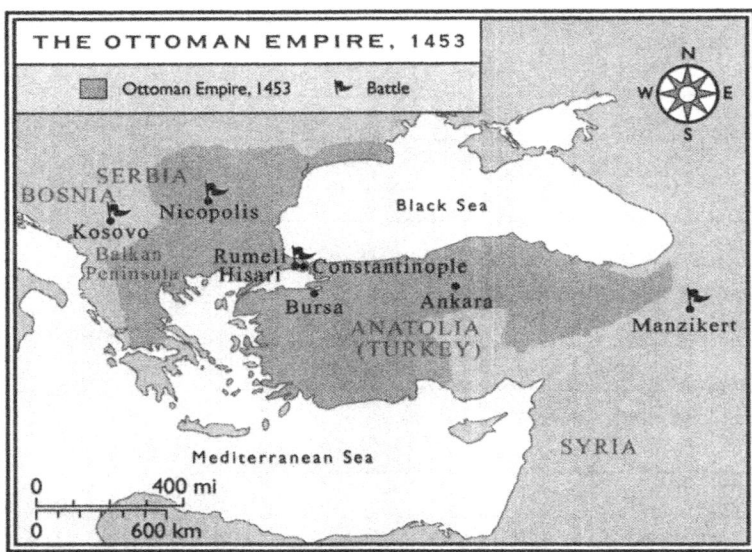

MAP LEGEND

CHAPTER 7

WHEN TENTS BECOME TOWERS: THE SULTANS SETTLE DOWN

CHAPTER SUMMARY

The Ottoman Empire flourished and expanded during the reign of the sultan Suleyman, and Istanbul was established as its capital city. After Suleyman's death, ineffective rulers and other difficulties began to weaken the empire.

ACCESS

Chapter 7 describes the expansion and development of the Ottoman Empire. Before you read the chapter, write down what you *know* about the Turks and the Ottoman Empire in the left column of the K-W-L chart. Then write what you *want to know* in the center column. After you have read the chapter, write what you *learned* in the last column.

K	W	L
What I Know	What I Want to Know	What I Learned
Islam was the official religion of the Ottoman Empire.	Did religious beliefs change as the empire expanded?	

CAST OF CHARACTERS

Briefly describe the role each character played in the Ottoman Empire.

Suleyman (soo-lay-MAHN) the Magnificent _____

Selim (she-LEEM) "the Grim" _____

Mimar (mee-MAHR) Sinan (see-NAHN) _____

Ahmet (ah-MEHT) III _____

WORD BANK

campaign   strait   siege   perimeter   succession

Choose words from the Word Bank to complete the sentences. One word is not used at all.

1. Fratricide was common in the Ottoman Empire in order to determine _____.

2. As a result of his successful military _____, Suleyman added lands to his empire.

3. Military leaders would often blockade cities during a _____.

4. Enemy ships could approach land by a narrow body of water called a _____.

WORD PLAY

Look up the word you did not use in the dictionary. Write a sentence using that word.

_____

_____

The prefix *peri-* means around. With a parent or partner, write down as many words beginning with *peri-* as you can think of in five minutes. Compare lists. Look up any words either of you does not know.

CRITICAL THINKING
SUMMARIZING

When you write a summary, you use your own words to briefly restate main ideas. To write a summary, identify the text's main ideas, and then write a statement that brings together the main ideas. Remember that a summary is always shorter than the original text.

Reread this passage from Chapter 7 about the sultan Suleyman. In your history journal, write a summary of its main ideas on the lines below.

> Suleyman saw himself as a man of order as well as a warrior. In Ottoman sources he is usually referred to as Suleyman the Law-Giver. One of the tasks he set for his reign was the creation of a legal system, bringing it up to date. These laws touched all parts of Ottoman life, including how much butter should be placed in pastry or how large a fine a man must pay for stealing a kiss from an unwilling woman. The purpose of the Kanun-i-Osman, the laws, was to prevent the "committing of acts of injustice" throughout the growing empire.

_____

_____

_____

_____

_____

WORKING WITH PRIMARY SOURCES

Reread this excerpt from the sidebar on Student Edition page 92. It is from a letter written in 1718 by Lady Mary Montagu, the wife of an English ambassador to the Turkish court.

> I live in a place that very well represents the Tower of Babel; in Pera [a suburb of Constantinople] they speak Turkish, Greek, Hebrew, Armenian, Arabic, Persian, Russian, Slovanian, Wallachian, German, Dutch, French, English, Italian, and what is worse, there is ten of these languages spoken in my own family. . . . I live in the perpetual hearing of this medley of sounds, which produces a very extraordinary effect upon the people who live here.

IDENTIFYING POINT OF VIEW

Lady Montagu's reference to the Tower of Babel comes from a story in the Old Testament in the Bible. In it, God prevents humans from building a tower by confusing their language so that they cannot communicate with each other.

1. Why does Lady Montagu compare Pera to the Tower of Babel?

2. What can you tell about Lady Montagu's attitude toward so many different peoples living in one place? Does she approve or disapprove? Use details from the excerpt to support your ideas.

3. What does Lady Montagu's writing reveal about how many languages she is familiar with?

4. How does Lady Montagu's writing reflect what you know about the Ottoman Empire?

WRITE ABOUT IT

In your history journal, write a short description that tells about a time when you were confused by something you had heard or seen. Include clear vivid words and images that help illustrate why you were confused.

ALL OVER THE MAP

Directions

Follow the steps below to complete the map.

- Draw a star on the capital city of the Ottoman Empire under Sultan Suleyman. Create a map legend and tell what this symbol represents.
- Use a color to circle the place of battle where Suleyman's victory became known as "the tomb of the Hungarian nation." Add this color to the map legend and tell what it represents.
- Use another color to circle the name of the Mediterranean island where Suleyman's forces defeated Christian crusaders. Add this color to the map legend and tell what it represents.
- Use another color to circle the name of the Mediterranean island that successfully fought off invasion by Suleyman's troops. Add this color to the map legend and tell what it represents.
- Use another color to circle the name of the European city where General Mustafa's failed siege ended in disaster for the Ottomans. Add this color to the map legend and tell what it represents.
- Give your map a title that explains what it shows.

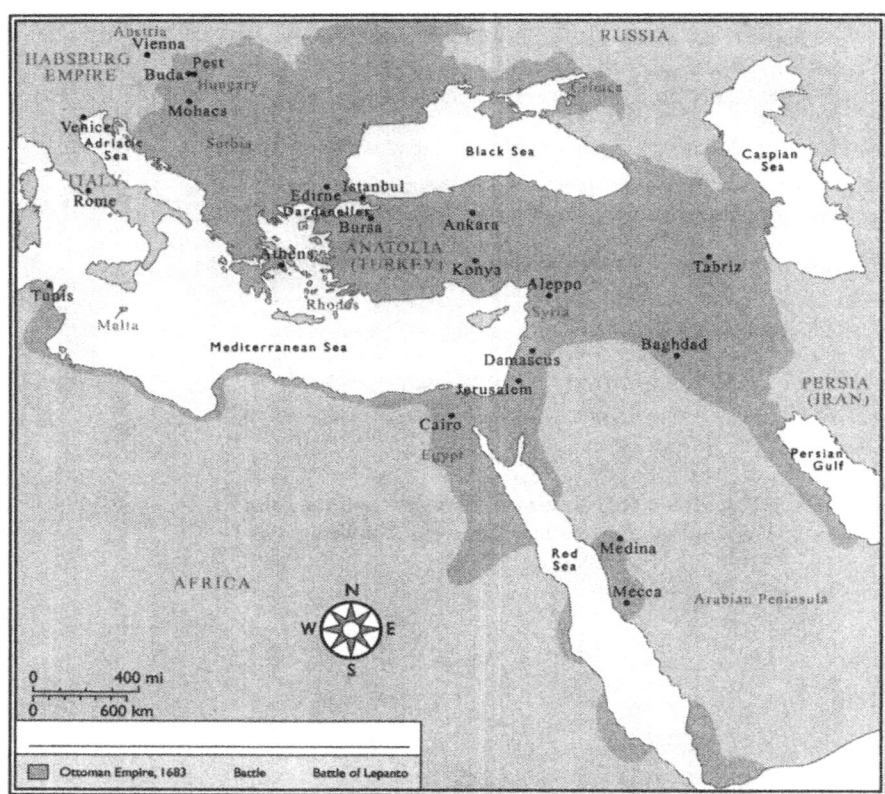

MAP LEGEND

38 CHAPTER 7

CHAPTER 8
STOCKING THE ROYAL SPICE CABINET: THE PORTUGUESE EMPIRE

CHAPTER SUMMARY

Exploration and naval power were keys to the building of the Portuguese empire and control of valuable trade routes in the 1400s and 1500s. Much of what the Portuguese gained was later lost, but many changes resulted from Portugal's contact with other parts of the world, both within and outside of the empire.

ACCESS

As you read Chapter 8, use the timeline graphic organizer to keep track of key dates and events in the building of the Portuguese empire. Connect each event to the appropriate place on the date line.

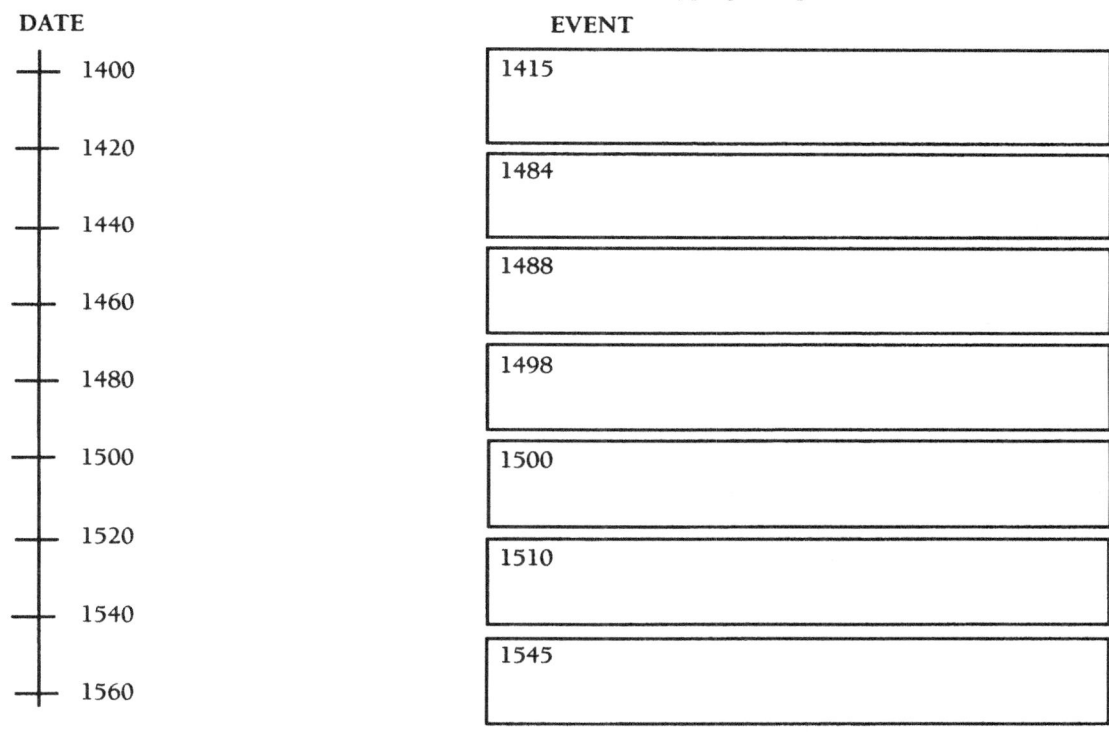

CAST OF CHARACTERS

State why each character was important.

Vasco (VAS-ko) Da Gama (duh GAH-mah) _____

_____

Bartolomeu (bahr-TAHL-AH-mew) Dias (DEE-ush) _____

_____

Henry "the Navigator" _____

_____

Philip II _____

_____

WORD BANK

navigator   exploration   crown   scurvy   treasuries   insurrections

Choose words from the Word Bank to complete the sentences. One word is not used at all.

1. Joao's forces fought Beatrice's forces for the _____ of Portugal.
2. Pedro Alvares Cabral was a Portuguese _____ who sighted Brazil.
3. A lack of vitamin C caused sailors to become ill with _____.
4. Gold and other riches were kept in the kings' _____.
5. Portugal gained its independence through _____ against its Spanish rulers.

WORD PLAY

Look up in a dictionary the word you did not use. Write a sentence using that word.

_____

CRITICAL THINKING
CAUSE AND EFFECT

Think about the causes and effects of Portuguese exploration and trade. Draw lines to match the "causes" in the left column with the "effects" in the right-hand column. (There is one extra effect.)

CAUSE	EFFECT
1. As a result of Henry the Navigator's gathering around him a group of mapmakers and men willing to take risks,	a. King Manuel I was nicknamed "The Fortunate."
2. As a result of Gil Eanes rounding Cape Bojador,	b. the Portuguese brought an estimated four million slaves to South America.
3. As a result of the Ottomans controlling the major spice routes to the East,	c. the Portuguese sailed further south along the coast of Africa.
4. As a result of the wealth coming to Portugal from Brazil,	d. the Portuguese exploration down the African coast began in 1415.
5. As a result of Portuguese violence and diseases introduced from Europe,	e. the American Indians suffered.
	f. the Inquisition spread to Portuguese colonies.
6. As a result of the transatlantic slave trade,	g. Henry the Navigator pushed to find an alternative trade route to the East.

WORKING WITH PRIMARY SOURCES

Read the sidebar on page 99, from the poem "The Luciads" in which the poet Luis de Camoes describes Portuguese exploration.

> Thus went we opening those seas,
> which save Our own no Nation open'd ere before,
> Seeing those new Isles and climates near which brave Prince Henry shewd unto the world before.

IDENTIFYING POINT OF VIEW

1. To whom do you think the word *we* referred? Explain.

2. Why do you think Luis de Camoes used the word *brave* to describe Prince Henry?

3. How do you think Luis de Camoes felt about Portugal? Explain.

WRITE ABOUT IT

Think of an accomplishment—whether your own or our country's—of which you are proud. In your history journal, write a poem or a paragraph to describe the accomplishment and explain why it makes you feel proud.

HISTORY JOURNAL

Don't forget to share your history journal with your classmates, and ask if you can see what their journals look like. You might be surprised—and get some new ideas.

ALL OVER THE MAP

Directions

Follow the steps below to complete the map.

- Scan pages 98–103 to find information about Portuguese exploration and trade.
- Make a list of the Portuguese explorers and navigators who led expeditions. Note the purpose of their trips and the routes they followed to reach their destinations.
- List the fortified cities for trade established by the Portuguese, note the date each was established, and note who established them.
- Choose a different color or patterned line to show the route each explorer or navigator took. For example, you might use a dotted line to show the route of one explorer, a dashed line to show the route of a second explorer, and a solid line to show the route of a third explorer.
- Show Lisbon as the starting point of each journey. Then draw each route where it belongs on the map.
- Add a date next to the route to show when the voyage occurred.
- Add a date to show when each fortified city for trade was established.
- Make a legend for your map showing what each route stands for.
- Give your map a title that explains what the map shows.

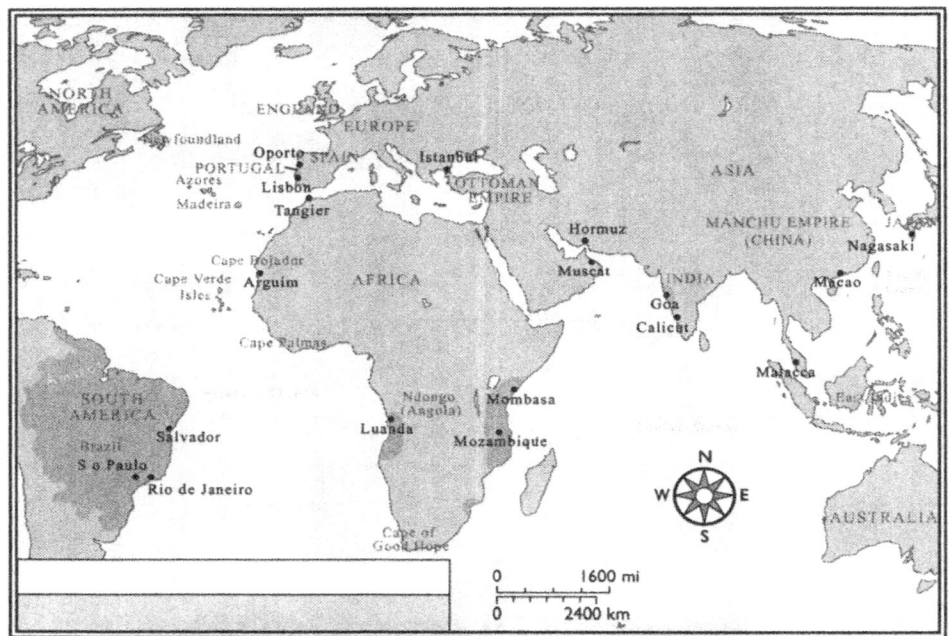

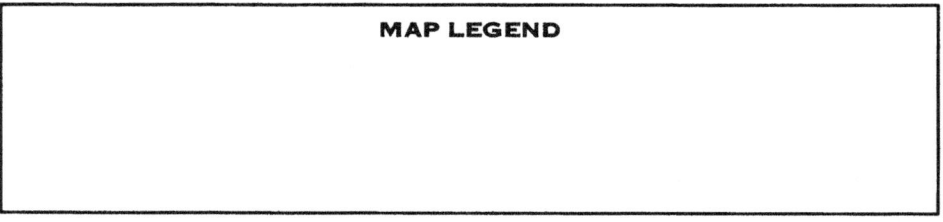

MAP LEGEND

CHAPTER 9
"GO FURTHER!": SPAIN EXPANDS ACROSS AN OCEAN

CHAPTER SUMMARY

The Catholic monarchy of Spain expanded its empire across the world and made Catholicism the dominant religion. Over time, the empire weakened because it did not develop its resources.

ACCESS

To organize information about the Spanish Empire, use the cause and effect chart. As you read each section, review the events, or causes, in the first column. Add the change, or effect, each event brought about in the second column.

CAUSE	EFFECT
1. Ferdinand and Isabella captured the city of Granada.	1.
2. Ferdinand and Isabella expelled Jews who refused to convert to Christianity.	2.
3. Christopher Columbus successfully explored the western Atlantic.	3.
4. Spanish monarchs were disturbed by the way Indian workers were treated.	4.
5. Native Americans had no resistance to European diseases.	5.
6. The Pueblo Indians did not like their treatment by the Europeans.	6.
7. Philip II wanted to stop William of Orange from spreading the Reformation.	7.
8. The English had better weapons and tactics than the Spanish Armada.	8.
9. The Spaniards squandered their money, did not develop resources, or support education.	9.

AN AGE OF EMPIRES, 1200–1750

CAST OF CHARACTERS

Tell how each person influenced the history of the Spanish Empire.

Isabella of Castile _____

_____

Ferdinand of Aragon _____

_____

Charles V _____

_____

Philip II _____

_____

Christopher Columbus _____

_____

WORD BANK

Iberian Peninsula   irrigation   Inquisition   trade winds   conquistadors   *conversos*

Choose words from the Word Bank to complete the sentences. One word is not used at all.

1. During the _____, religious trials were held to see if people were following Catholic beliefs.

2. Spies checked to make sure that the _____ did not follow Jewish practices.

3. Columbus used the _____ to cross the Atlantic.

4. Portugal and Spain are located on the _____.

5. The Muslims in Spain used _____ techniques to bring water to crops.

WORD PLAY

Look up the word that you did not use in the dictionary. What is the root word and its meaning?

_____

WITH A PARENT OR PARTNER

Choose one of the vocabulary words and build a word web like the one below with it in your history journal. Include related words and phrases. Have a parent or partner do the same. Share your word webs and note similarities and differences.

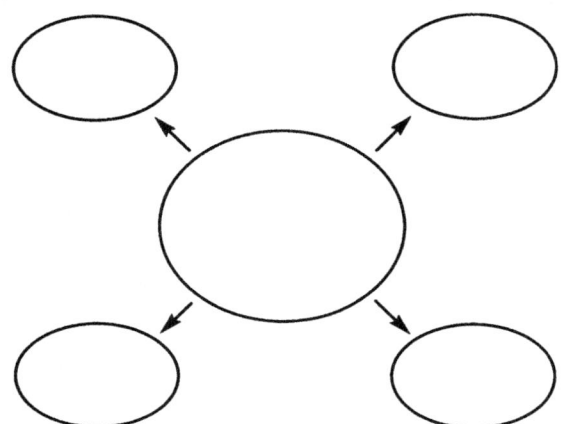

CRITICAL THINKING
DRAWING CONCLUSIONS

A conclusion is an understanding about what you have read. As shown below, to draw a conclusion, use what you already know along with what you read.

DETAILS FROM THE CHAPTER	WHAT I KNOW	CONCLUSION
The *moriscos* were moved from Granada and scattered over Spain.	People who are forcibly moved often lose their property and their ties to their community.	The *moriscos* most likely struggled financially and emotionally after their move.

In your history journal, make a similar chart to draw a conclusion about another group that was forcibly displaced by the Spaniards.

WORKING WITH PRIMARY SOURCES
IDENTIFYING POINT OF VIEW

Philip II lived from 1527 to 1598. He governed from his palace on the plains outside Madrid, Spain. He relied on a system of councils in different parts of the empire. The councils were responsible to the Council of State. The Council of State provided Philip with advice, but he made the final decisions. Every document needed the king's signature.

Read the quotation from the caption on Student Edition page 109. It is an excerpt from a letter by a Catholic missionary in America, sent to Philip II in Spain.

> Your Majesty is like a blind man who has excellent understanding, but can only see exterior objects through the eyes of those who describe them to you.

1. How would you describe the tone of the missionary's letter to Philip?

2. Why do you think the missionary compares Philip to a blind man?

3. Does this quotation express an opinion or a fact? How can you tell?

4. What do you know about Philip's life that supports the missionary's statement?

WRITE ABOUT IT

The missionary uses a simile to describe Philip II. On the lines below, write a simile about another ruler or explorer described in the chapter, such as Christopher Columbus or Queen Isabella. Read it aloud to a partner, and explain its meaning.

ALL OVER THE MAP

Directions

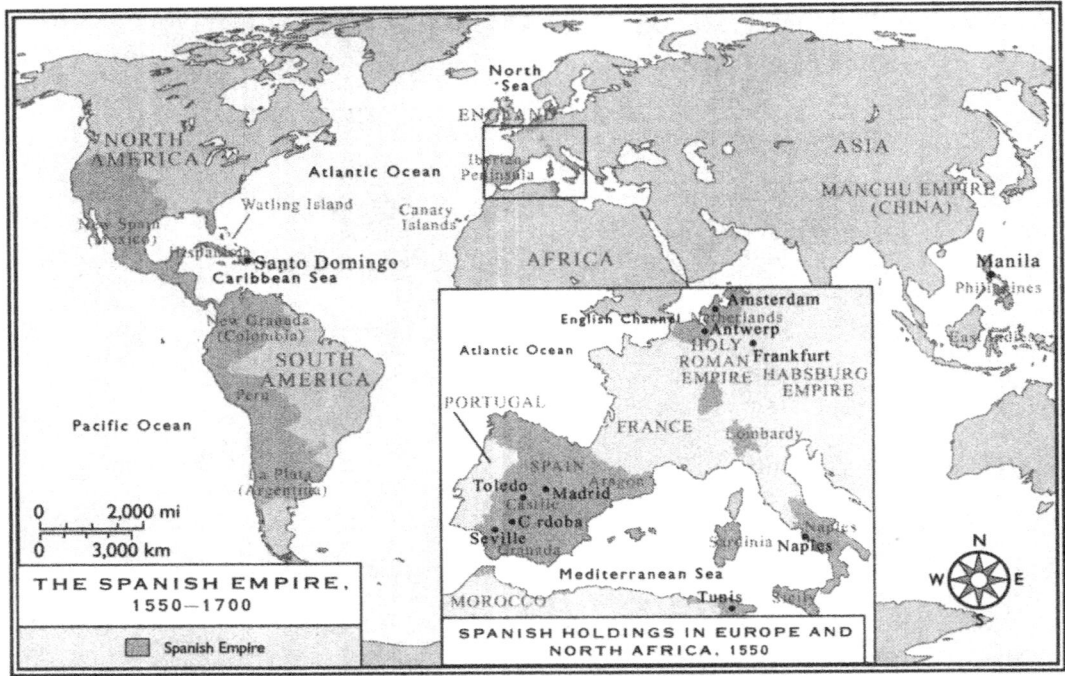

Follow the steps below to complete the map. Then answer the question that follows.

- Scan the chapter to find information about battles, forced expulsions, and conquests.
- Make a list of the events and dates.
- Make a small icon for each event you wish to place on the map. For example, a small flame can indicate a battle.
- Draw each icon on the map, with the dates.
- Add an arrow for each icon that indicates a movement, such as the movement of enslaved people from Africa to the Americas.
- Make a legend for your map showing what each icon stands for.

Draw conclusions about the tensions within the empire, based on your map.

_____
_____
_____
_____
_____
_____
_____

CHAPTER 10
THE WEDDING RING EMPIRE: EUROPE UNDER THE HABSBURGS

CHAPTER SUMMARY
The Habsburg Empire used royal weddings to rule over parts of Central Europe for 500 years. Their devotion to Catholicism was the source of ever-deepening religious conflict.

ACCESS
To help you organize information about the Habsburg Empire, complete the timeline below. As you read the chapter, add events and details to the timeline. Draw lines to connect each event to its place on the timeline.

TIMELINE

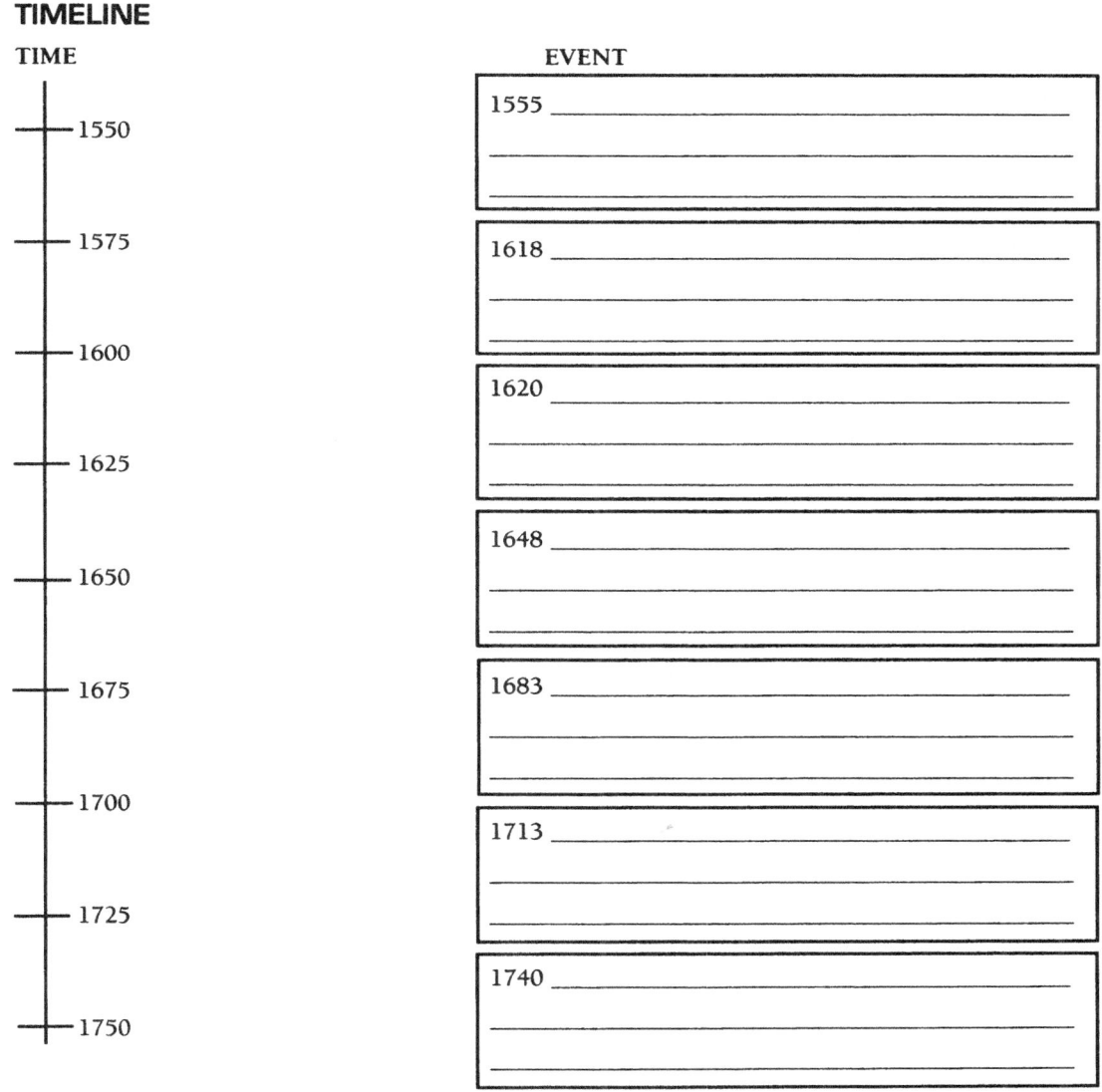

AN AGE OF EMPIRES, 1200–1750   **47**

CAST OF CHARACTERS

Describe the role each character played in the Habsburg Empire.

Johannes Kepler _____

General Albrecht von Wallenstein _____

Eugene of Savoy _____

Maria Theresa _____

WORD BANK

assassins holdings discrimination mercenary insignia traits elliptical paths

Choose words or terms from the Word Bank to complete the sentences. One word is not used at all.

1. The Habsburg Empire grew from family _____ that were originally located in Switzerland.

2. During the Thirty Years' War, General Wallenstein used a vast number of _____ fighters to battle German states and their allies.

3. Members of families often resemble one another through shared physical _____.

4. Johannes Kepler determined that planetary orbits follow _____.

5. Planned murders of public officials are carried out by _____.

6. Many Protestants faced _____ under the rule of the Catholic Habsburgs.

WORD PLAY

Look up the word you did not use in the dictionary. Write a sentence using that word, and include an example of its meaning.

_____

WITH A PARENT OR PARTNER

The word *traits* can also refer to personality characteristics. With a parent or partner, make a list of personality traits that you think are necessary for a good leader. Then make a list of current national and local leaders and discuss which of the traits you listed they possess.

CRITICAL THINKING

IDENTIFYING MAIN IDEA AND DETAILS

Reread the passage from Chapter 10 that describes the Habsburg Empire. Then complete the chart with details from the chapter that support these ideas.

> From 1500 to 1750, the Habsburgs had three main problems: dealing with the Reformation, defeating the Ottomans, and ensuring a peaceful succession of power.

MAIN IDEA	DETAILS
1. The Habsburgs had to deal with the Reformation.	
2. The Habsburgs had to defeat the Ottomans.	
3. The Habsburgs had to ensure a peaceful succession of power.	

WORKING WITH PRIMARY SOURCES

DRAWING CONCLUSIONS

Answer the following questions to draw conclusions about Maria Theresa. Explain your answers using complete sentences.

The following quotations appear on Student Edition pages 128 and 130. Reread the quotations from Maria Theresa about her father, Charles VI, her succession to his throne, and her opinion of the Prussians.

> It never pleased my father's Majesty to have me present when he transacted business, domestic or foreign.

> I do not think anyone would deny that history hardly knows of a crowned head who started his rule under circumstances more grievous than those attending my accession.

> You had better realize that no one is to be trusted less than the Prussians.

1. Do you think Maria Theresa felt that she was ready to take the throne and rule the Habsburg Empire?

2. Do you think that Maria Theresa felt sorry for herself, or that she wanted others to feel sorry for her?

3. What do her remarks about the Prussians reveal about her?

4. Which of the quotations give the best indication of Maria Theresa's leadership skills? Explain your choice.

WRITE ABOUT IT

Maria Theresa faced a great challenge: taking the throne and ruling the Habsburg Empire. In your history journal, write a paragraph about a time when you were faced with a challenge. Explain why you saw the upcoming event or situation as a challenge. Tell whether or how you prepared for the challenge.

ALL OVER THE MAP

Directions

Follow the steps below to complete the map.

- Choose an icon, such as a star, an X, or a flag, that will indicate a site or place showing threats to the Habsburg Empire. You will need to use four different colors when using this icon on the map.
- Place an icon on the site of the Czech rebellion in the early 1600s that led to the Thirty Years' War.
- Place another icon on the place that the Ottoman Empire tried to capture from the Habsburgs in 1683.
- Place another icon next to the name of the country that was freed from Ottoman rule, but then revolted under Habsburg rule.
- Place another icon next to the place that the Prussians invaded following the death of Charles VI.
- Make a legend for your map showing what each icon stands for.
- Give your map a title that explains what it shows.

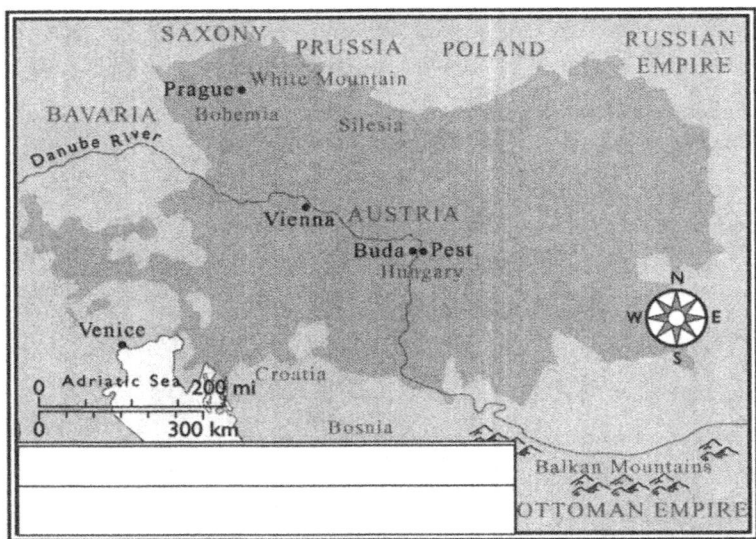

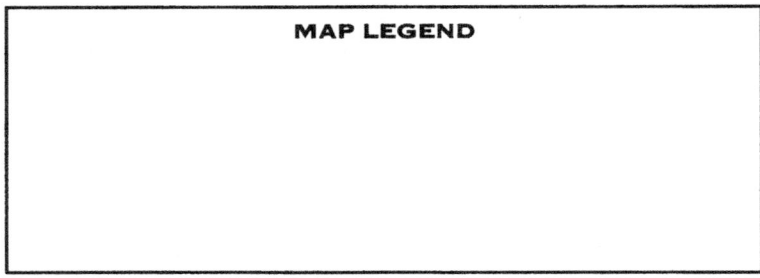

MAP LEGEND

CHAPTER 11: TEENAGERS TAKE THE THRONE: MANCHU CHINA

CHAPTER SUMMARY

The Manchus of northeastern China began the Qing dynasty. They tried to keep their culture intact while ruling the Chinese majority. At the height of the dynasty, the Qing rulers supported education and trade and expanded China's borders.

ACCESS

Chapter 11 tells about the Qing Dynasty of China, which was led by the Manchus of northeastern China. As you read the chapter, review the main ideas in the outline below. Add details that support the main idea on the lines provided.

MAIN IDEA: The Manchus faced challenges when they took over the empire from the Ming Dynasty.

DETAIL: _____

DETAIL: _____

DETAIL: _____

MAIN IDEA: Manchu leaders tried to support their culture and keep it separate.

DETAIL: _____

DETAIL: _____

DETAIL: _____

MAIN IDEA: Kangxi and Qianlong led China in years of prosperity.

DETAIL: _____

DETAIL: _____

DETAIL: _____

AN AGE OF EMPIRES, 1200–1750

CAST OF CHARACTERS

Write a sentence explaining how Kangxi's rule influenced the rule of Qianlong.

_____
_____
_____

WORD BANK

Use each pair of words in parentheses in a sentence about the chapter.

1. (dynasty, administration) _____
2. (custom, deity) _____
3. (Buddhist, Confucian) _____

WORD PLAY

Look up *dynasty* in the dictionary. What is the root word and its meaning?

_____

WITH A PARENT OR PARTNER

Discuss one of the ways in which the Manchu minority tried to protect its culture. Brainstorm ways in which minority groups in your community try to teach their culture to future generations as well as share it with others.

CRITICAL THINKING
MAKING COMPARISONS AND CONTRASTS

To make a comparison, look for how two things are alike. To make a contrast, look for how two things are different. Words that signal comparisons include *similar*, *both*, and *the same as*. Words that signal contrasts include *however*, *on the other hand*, and *but*. Look at these examples from the chapter.

COMPARISON	CONTRAST
Not only were Shunzi and Kangxi young, they were not even Chinese, but Manchus, a separate group of people from northeastern China. (page 133)	Qianlong tried to model himself after Kangxi, but he did not have the same sense of balance that his grandfather had. (page 141)

1. How did the author compare or contrast each pair of emperors?

_____
_____

2. How does this writing technique help you understand what they were like?

_____
_____

In your history journal, write an explanatory paragraph in which you compare and contrast aspects of Manchu and Chinese culture, economics, or government. Include important details from the chapter.

WORKING WITH PRIMARY SOURCES

IDENTIFYING POINT OF VIEW

The Manchu built military forts in strategic cities in key Chinese provinces. Although the Manchu had their own soldiers, they appointed Chinese military leaders to command Chinese troops.

Read the sidebar quotation of Kangxi, the second Qing emperor, from Student Edition page 140. Then answer the questions below.

> There's an old saying that if the civilian officers don't seek money and the military officials aren't afraid of death, we need never fear that the country won't have Great Peace.

1. What is the topic of Kangxi's quotation?

2. What do you think Kangxi wanted his civilian officers and military officers to be like?

3. Why do you think Kangxi had to pay attention to military matters throughout China?

4. Why do you think Kangxi had both Manchu and ethnic Chinese as military leaders?

WRITE ABOUT IT

Emperor Kangxi frequently toured his lands and visited his troops. It was one way to avoid problems later. He wrote, "Stirring up trouble is not as good as preventing trouble from happening." In your history journal, write a journal entry from the point of view of Kangxi. Describe an encounter he has with a military leader during one of his inspections in China.

ALL OVER THE MAP

Directions

Follow the steps below to complete the map.

- Imagine you are a trader in 1750. You need to get your goods to major markets in China. Your route can include land and water routes.
- On the lines below write five questions about the distances that you might travel. Write the answers to your questions on a separate sheet of paper.
- Exchange your questions with a partner to solve using the scale of miles.
- Compare your answers to your partner's and decide if any answers need to be corrected.

1. _____

2. _____

3. _____

4. _____

5. _____

Draw conclusions about the routes along the Silk Road, based on your map.

_____
_____
_____
_____
_____

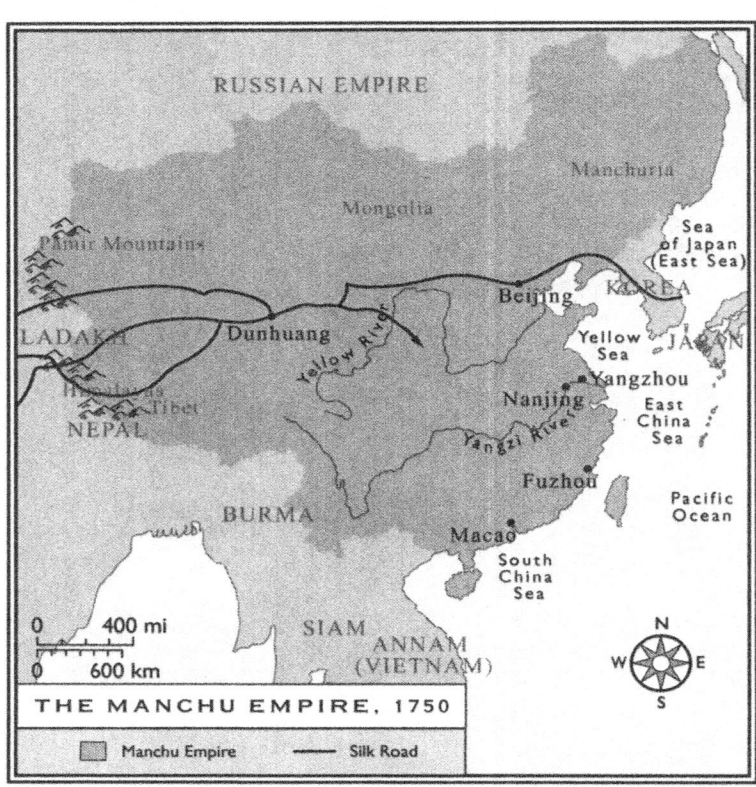

THE MANCHU EMPIRE, 1750

NAME _____   DUE DATE _____

LIBRARY/ MEDIA CENTER RESEARCH LOG

What I Need to Find

I need to use:
- ☐ primary
- ☐ secondary

_____ sources.

Places I Know to Look

Brainstorm: Other Sources and Places to Look

WHAT I FOUND

Title/Author/Location (call # or URL)

Title/Author/Location	Book/Periodical	Website	Other	Primary Source	Secondary Source	How I Found it (Suggestion / Library Catalog / Browsing / Internet Search / Web link)	Rate each source from 1 (low) to 4 (high) in the categories below — helpful / relevant
_____	☐	☐	☐	☐	☐	☐☐☐☐☐	____ ____
_____	☐	☐	☐	☐	☐	☐☐☐☐☐	____ ____
_____	☐	☐	☐	☐	☐	☐☐☐☐☐	____ ____
_____	☐	☐	☐	☐	☐	☐☐☐☐☐	____ ____
_____	☐	☐	☐	☐	☐	☐☐☐☐☐	____ ____
_____	☐	☐	☐	☐	☐	☐☐☐☐☐	____ ____

NAME _____

LIBRARY / MEDIA CENTER RESEARCH LOG

DUE DATE _____

What I Need to Find

[   ]

I need to use: [   ]
☐ primary ____ sources.
☐ secondary

Places I Know to Look

[   ]

Brainstorm: Other Sources and Places to Look

[   ]

WHAT I FOUND

Title/Author/Location (call # or URL)

Title/Author/Location	Book/Periodical	Website	Other	Primary Source	Secondary Source	How I Found it (Suggestion / Library Catalog / Browsing / Internet Search / Web link)	helpful	relevant
_____	☐	☐	☐	☐	☐	☐☐☐☐☐	____	____
_____	☐	☐	☐	☐	☐	☐☐☐☐☐	____	____
_____	☐	☐	☐	☐	☐	☐☐☐☐☐	____	____
_____	☐	☐	☐	☐	☐	☐☐☐☐☐	____	____
_____	☐	☐	☐	☐	☐	☐☐☐☐☐	____	____
_____	☐	☐	☐	☐	☐	☐☐☐☐☐	____	____

Rate each source from 1 (low) to 4 (high) in the categories below

NAME

LIBRARY/ MEDIA CENTER RESEARCH LOG

DUE DATE

What I Need to Find

I need to use:
- ☐ primary
- ☐ secondary

sources.

Places I Know to Look

Brainstorm: Other Sources and Places to Look

WHAT I FOUND

Title/Author/Location (call # or URL)

_____

_____

_____

_____

_____

_____

Book/Periodical	Website	Other		Primary Source	Secondary Source		Suggestion	Library Catalog	Browsing	Internet Search	Web link		**Rate each source from 1 (low) to 4 (high) in the categories below**	
						How I Found it						helpful	relevant
☐	☐	☐		☐	☐		☐	☐	☐	☐	☐	_____	_____
☐	☐	☐		☐	☐		☐	☐	☐	☐	☐	_____	_____
☐	☐	☐		☐	☐		☐	☐	☐	☐	☐	_____	_____
☐	☐	☐		☐	☐		☐	☐	☐	☐	☐	_____	_____
☐	☐	☐		☐	☐		☐	☐	☐	☐	☐	_____	_____
☐	☐	☐		☐	☐		☐	☐	☐	☐	☐	_____	_____

NAME _____

LIBRARY/ MEDIA CENTER RESEARCH LOG

DUE DATE _____

What I Need to Find

Brainstorm: Other Sources and Places to Look

Places I Know to Look

I need to use:
- ☐ primary
- ☐ secondary

sources.

WHAT I FOUND

Title/Author/Location (call # or URL)

How I Found it
- Suggestion
- Library Catalog
- Browsing
- Internet Search
- Web link

Rate each source from 1 (low) to 4 (high) in the categories below

helpful   relevant

Columns (checkboxes per row): Book/Periodical ☐ | Website ☐ | Other ☐ | Primary Source ☐ | Secondary Source ☐ | Suggestion ☐ | Library Catalog ☐ | Browsing ☐ | Internet Search ☐ | Web link ☐ | helpful ___ | relevant ___

(6 source entry rows)

Printed in Dunstable, United Kingdom